HAMPSHIRE
NEW FO[

C000175788

Teashop Walks

Jean Patefield

COUNTRYSIDE BOOKS
NEWBURY BERKSHIRE

First published 1998
© Jean Patefield 1998

Reprinted 1999
Revised and updated 2002

COUNTRYSIDE BOOKS
3 Catherine Road
Newbury, Berkshire

ISBN 1 85306 500 5

Designed by Graham Whiteman
Cover illustration by Colin Doggett
Photographs and maps by the author

Produced through MRM Associates Ltd., Reading
Typeset by Techniset Typesetters, Newton-le-Willows
Printed by J. W. Arrowsmith Ltd., Bristol

Contents

Walk

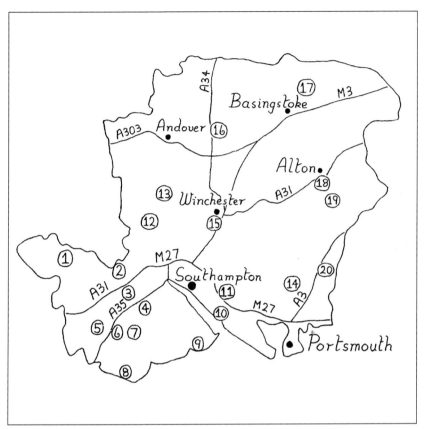

Area map showing the locations of the walks.

KEY TO SKETCH MAPS

Path on route — — →	Sea or river estuary ~ ~ ~	Point in text ⑥
Path not on route ...	Church †	Car park ▫
Road ═══	Teashop	Building or feature referred to in text ▪
River or stream ∿∿∿	Pub refered to in text PH	Railway ++++++
		Bridge ⎵

Introduction

Hampshire has much to offer the walker with a surprisingly wide variety of landscapes to enjoy. This is a county of rolling downland, ancient forests, airy and heathery heaths threaded by sparkling trout streams wending their way through green water meadows. It is also a coastal county, famed throughout the world for its ports and overlooking one of the busiest shipping lanes in the world where all types of craft from dinghies to mighty tankers add interest to seaside walks.

The 20 walks described in this book aim to give a taste of all the landscapes making up this most English of counties. They are all between 2½ and 8 miles and should be well within the capacity of the average person, including those of mature years and families with children. They are intended to take the walker through this attractive corner of England at a gentle pace with plenty of time to stop and stare, to savour the beauty and interest all around. A dedicated yomper and stomper could probably knock off the whole book in a single weekend but in doing so they would have missed the point and seen nothing. To fully appreciate the countryside it is necessary to go slowly with your eyes and ears open.

Certain of the walks involve some climbing. This is inevitable as hills add enormous interest to the countryside and with no hills there are no views. However, this presents no problem to the sensible walker who has three uphill gears - slowly, very slowly and admiring the view. None of the walks in this book are inherently hazardous but sensible care should be taken.

All the routes are on public rights of way or permissive paths and have been carefully checked but, of course, in the countryside things do change; a gate is replaced by a stile or a wood is extended. Each walk is circular and is illustrated by a sketch map. An Ordnance Survey map is useful as well, especially for identifying the main features of views. The area is covered by Landranger 1:50 000 (1¼ inches to 1 mile) series, sheets 184, 185, 186, 195, 196 and 197. In addition, the New Forest is covered by the very useful 1:25 000 Outdoor Leisure map 22 and there are also the Pathfinder 1:25 000 maps, each of which covers a small area. The grid reference of the starting point and the number of the appropriate Landranger map are given for each walk.

The walks are designed so that, starting where suggested, the teashop is reached in the second half so a really good appetite for tea can be worked up and then its effects walked off. Some walks start at a car park, which is ideal. Where this is not possible, the suggested starting place will always have somewhere where a few cars can be left without endangering other traffic or causing inconvenience. However, it sometimes fits in better with the plans for the day to start and finish at the teashop and so for each walk there are details of how to do this.

Tea is often said to be the best meal to eat out in England and I believe that it is something to be enjoyed on all possible occasions. Scones with cream and strawberry jam, delicious home-made cakes, toasted teacakes dripping with butter in winter, delicate cucumber sandwiches in summer, all washed down with the cup that cheers. Bad for the figure maybe, but the walking will see to that.

The best teashops serve a range of cakes, all home-made and including fruit cake as well as scones and other temptations. Also, teapots should be capacious and pour properly. Most of the teashops visited on these walks fulfil all these criteria admirably and they all offer a good tea. They always have at least light lunches available as well so there is no need to think of these walks as just something for the afternoons.

The pleasures of summer walking are obvious. Many of the teashops featured in this book have an attractive garden where tea can be taken outside when the weather is suitable. However, let me urge you not to overlook the pleasures of a good walk in winter. The roads and paths are quieter and what could be better than sitting by an open fire in a cosy teashop scoffing crumpets that you can enjoy with a clear conscience due to the brisk walk to get them!

Teashops are not scattered evenly throughout Hampshire. In some places popular with tourists, the visitor is spoilt for choice. In such cases the teashop that, in the author's opinion, most closely fulfils the criteria set out above is recommended but should that not appeal, there are others from which to choose. In other places where there is a delightful walk to be enjoyed the choice for tea may be more limited. However, all the establishments offer a good tea partway round an attractive walk. The opening times and telephone number of each teashop are given. Some are rather vague about when they open out of season: it seems to depend on weather and mood. If you are planning a walk on a wet November Tuesday, for example, a call to check that tea will actually be available that day is a wise precaution. A few are definitely closed in the depths of winter and for these walks an alternative source of refreshment is given. In most cases, these are pubs serving food, which sometimes includes tea.

So put on your walking shoes and prepare to be delighted by the charms of Hampshire and a traditional English tea!

Jean Patefield

Walk 1
BREAMORE

This is a walk through a landscape steeped in history. It starts at the church in Breamore (pronounced Bremmer) which has stood unaltered since before the Conquest. It soon passes the 16th-century Breamore House and climbs to a mysterious monument, enjoying views to an Iron Age fort across the valley. The route then descends to the valley to pick up an ancient path back to Breamore and tea at the Countryside Museum. Do not be surprised if some parts seem familiar: this is a favourite spot with film and television producers in search of period atmosphere. For example, 'The Woodlanders' and 'Children of the New Forest' were both made here.

 Breamore House Tea Room offers a tasty selection of cakes and other teatime goodies such as toasted teacakes, flapjacks and clotted cream teas. It has ample indoor accommodation and some tables outside, overlooking a courtyard. From May to September it is open every day except Monday and

Friday and in August it is open daily. It also opens all bank holidays, Easter weekend and Tuesday, Wednesday and Sunday in April. The opening hours are from noon until 5.30 pm. For lunch, sandwiches, filled jacket potatoes, ploughman's and a selection of salads are served. Telephone: 01725 329746.

There is no other source of refreshment on the walk.

DISTANCE: 4 miles.

MAP: OS Landranger 184 Salisbury and The Plain.

STARTING POINT: Breamore church (GR 153188).

HOW TO GET THERE: Follow the signs to Breamore church from Breamore on the A338, the Salisbury to Fordingbridge road, 2 miles north of Fordingbridge. Having turned off the main road where signed, bear right at a fork after about $1/4$ mile, then right again to the church.

ALTERNATIVE STARTING POINT: The teashop is very near the starting point for this walk. To visit it before setting out, do not turn right to Breamore House but go straight ahead and the teashop is on the left.

THE WALK

St Mary's church has survived almost intact from Saxon times and has several features of interest, fully described in the guide book available within. These include three mass dials, a small one at the west angle of the porch and two more on quoins at the south-east angle of the transept. A mass dial is a stone with a hole to take a stick. There are scratches to act as a sundial and it was a primitive timepiece to enable the priest to know when to say mass in the days before clocks.

1. With your back to the church, bear right to the entrance to Breamore House. Turn right along the drive, signed as a bridleway, passing the house on the right.

Breamore House was built in 1583 and has the 'E' shape characteristic of Elizabethan buildings. It was bought by Sir Edward Hulse, physician to Queen Anne, George I and George II in the 18th century and remains the home of the Hulse family. The interior was damaged by fire in 1856 but it still contains many important pictures and pieces of furniture. It is open the same times of year as the teashop from 2 pm until 5.30 pm and tickets to visit the house can be obtained near the teashop.

2. Pass the house, and go ahead on a track up into and through Breamore Wood, ignoring all side turnings. On leaving the wood, continue along the track, joining another coming in from the right.

9

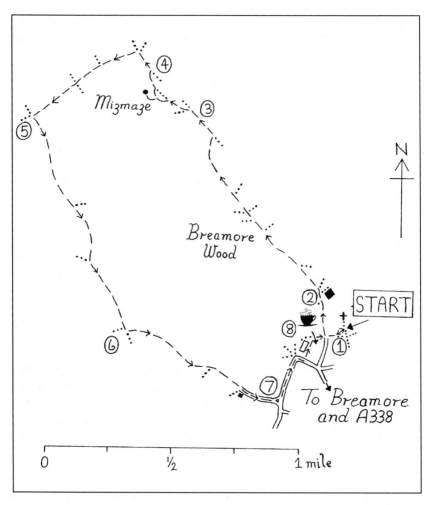

This peaceful agricultural scene is a landscape full of history. To the left is Whitsbury where there was a hilltop Iron Age fort covering some 16 acres, whose earthen ramparts can still be seen. Beyond that at Rockbourne, out of sight in a sheltered valley, is a 2nd century Roman villa. To the right, local tradition tells of a great battle fought in AD 519 between Saxon invaders commanded by Cerdic and the Britons under the King, Natan-Leod, when 5,000 of the latter, including the king, were killed.

3. When the hedges on both sides of the track end, take the centre one of three paths ahead, towards a sign for the Mizmaze. Follow the path left through the wood to the monument. Return to the sign and continue left along the path, soon joining a path coming in from the right.

This turf maze is one of only two in Hampshire, the other being on St Catherine's Hill visited on walk 15. It is not at all what we usually think of as a maze, which has hedged, blind ended paths and originated in Tudor times. Turf mazes are earlier and are similar to stone ones found on the Continent. They are not a puzzle but said to be full of Christian symbolism. This example is a continuous turf path within a circle 80 feet in diameter and may have been connected with an Augustinian monastery near Breamore. The monastery was suppressed in 1536 and now no trace of it remains.

4. At a cross track in front of a hedge turn left for about 100 yards. Cross a stile on the left, opposite a grassy track on the right, and walk down the left-hand side of a field. At the end of the field, continue ahead into woodland and then on in the same direction at a cross track, eventually arriving at a stile by a field gate.

5. Immediately over the stile, turn left along a cross track for about a mile, ignoring tracks on the left and right to farms.

6. Turn left on a signed footpath along the right-hand side of a field. (This is about 35 yards after a bridleway on the right.) This ancient path, which led to the neighbouring village of Whitsbury, is soon obviously sunken below the level of the field. At the end of the field, cross a stile and continue on the path. Eventually, by a picturesque thatched cottage, this becomes a surfaced lane.

7. Turn left at a T junction, passing more picture postcard houses. Some 70 yards after a right-hand bend turn left to Breamore House car park, museum and tea room.

The entrance to Breamore House is by the teashop. The interesting Countryside Museum has been created in a farmyard. It gives a fascinating glimpse of life in the village in days gone by with reconstructions of, for example, a village blacksmith's, a school and a labourer's cottage. It is open the same days as the teashop between 1 pm and 5.30 pm.

8. Turn right behind the tea room, back to the start.

Walk 2
BRAMSHAW WOOD

This route explores an outstanding area of ancient woodland in the quieter north of the New Forest and is of considerable ecological interest. It climbs to the highest point of the Forest and fine views reward this short but quite energetic walk. It is almost entirely on forest paths and is highly recommended.

Bramble Hill Hotel was a royal hunting lodge until 1851 when it was taken over by the first Sir William Glyn, of banking fame, and developed into a private residence. It became a hotel in 1954. Teas, including delicious cakes and cream teas with clotted cream, are served every afternoon between 2.30 pm and 5.30 pm from Easter to the end of October and at weekends in winter. At lunchtime there is an extensive bar menu and some very tempting desserts such as lemon brûlé and tiramisu. There are tables on the lawn in a very attractive garden. Telephone: 02380 813165.

There is no other source of refreshment on this walk.

DISTANCE: 3½ miles.

MAP: OS Landranger 184 Salisbury and The Plain.

STARTING POINT: Bramshaw Wood car park (GR 257173).

HOW TO GET THERE: From the B3079 (the road from Landford on the A36 to junction 1 on the M27), just inside the Forest boundary to the south of Landford take a minor road west to Bramshaw Wood car park on the left.

ALTERNATIVE STARTING POINT: If you wish to visit the teashop at the beginning or end of your walk, start at Bramble Hill Hotel where permission should be sought before leaving your car for a period. You will then start the walk at point 9. Take a path from the hotel drive, signed by a finger post, and follow the signed path to a gate into the forest then go uphill a short distance.

THE WALK

1. Go through the wooden posts at the rear of the car park and take the clear path ahead. Follow this downhill with shortly a bank on the right (an old inclosure boundary) to a cross path and a small clearing through which a stream runs. Note that the pebbly bed of the stream may sometimes be dry.

2. Cross the stream and take an obvious uphill path on the other side that forks after a few yards. Take this, bearing right at the fork and still following the bank on the right. Bear right again at the next fork and continue to a stream - in fact the same stream but now a more obvious feature.

3. Over the stream turn left, leaving the inclosure bank. Follow the path uphill.

There are some fine beech trees in this area. Beech is a lovely tree with smooth grey bark and glossy green leaves. It is especially beautiful in the spring, when the newly emerged leaves are so fresh, and in autumn, when they change from gold to orange to brown. Southern England is the northernmost extent of the beech's range: individual trees are found further north but there are no extensive beech woods. The fruit of the beech, sometimes called mast, is a three sided nut enclosed in a capsule with quite soft prickles on the outside. Fruit in quantity is produced only in irregular so-called mast years, sometimes at quite long intervals. In other years a late spring frost interferes with the setting of the nuts or a cool summer prevents their ripening. This is one reason why oak is the dominant tree in most of Britain. Beech has such a dense canopy that it absorbs a lot of the light and not much can grow below it, so the forest beneath beech is very open.

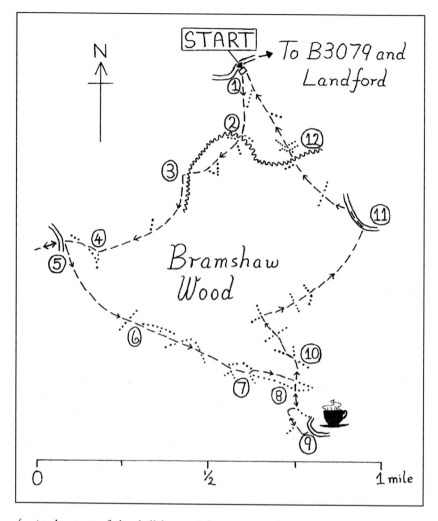

4. At the top of the hill bear right to a road.

This is Pipers Wait - the highest point of the New Forest at 422 feet. It is worth going ahead, across the road to the edge of the slope, for an excellent view across to Bramshaw Telegraph to the west and over Wiltshire to the north. Bramshaw Telegraph was one of a chain of semaphore signalling stations established during the Napoleonic War, when there was a real fear of invasion. Its main purpose was to transmit intelligence and orders to and from Portsmouth to naval units working from west country ports.

14

5. Immediately before the road turn left on a path across the heath. The path soon becomes more obvious and has extensive views to the left and heads towards trees.

One heathland resident is the adder, the only poisonous British snake. Adders like dry, sunny areas such as the heaths but there is no need to be nervous; they are in far more danger from your crashing boots than you are from them. Usually they will sense vibrations in the ground long before you get near, and slither off out of harm's way into the undergrowth. It is very rare for any one to be bitten and is almost always never fatal.

6. Fork right into woodland and follow the clear, main path, ignoring all side turns, for a good ¼ mile.

7. Eventually, a sign suggests walkers bear left and horses go straight on (though the New Forest ponies don't take much notice!). Follow the walkers' path, which soon joins a path coming in from the left.

☕ **8.** After about 200 yards, watch out for a metal gate and buildings glimpsed through trees to the right. Walk down towards them and pass though the gate. Follow the clearly signed path to the hotel and tea.

9. Retrace your steps to the gate and follow a path uphill to a fork with a horse/walker sign similar to that passed earlier. Bear right on the walker's path to continue uphill then down to a cross path.

10. Turn left for 50 yards then turn right to continue downhill. Go over a faint cross path and continue down to a second, rather more clear cross path. Turn right and follow the path to a road, ignoring all cross paths. At times, especially as it approaches the road, the path may become fainter but press on in the same direction.

11. Turn left along the road for 100 yards to a bar gate by some wooden posts. Turn left and follow the path round to the right and over a cross path after about 150 yards. The path is now more obvious and leads to a plank footbridge.

12. Some 25 yards after the bridge the path starts to rise. Follow the initially sunken path uphill, ignoring two cross paths close together. Continue uphill in the same direction when a path joins on the right and you are soon back at the car park.

Walk 3
ACRES DOWN

The New Forest has many attractive walks but this one is in a class of its own – and it saves the best until last! It starts at Millyford Bridge just outside Emery Down and visits the site of an unusual relic of recent history. The route is then mainly on well made tracks and climbs very gently. For most of the way the ascent is so gradual that you barely notice it. After tea in the garden of Acres Down Farm a final few feet of climbing brings you out on the wide, airy plateau of Acres Down with outstanding views, especially south and west. Having enjoyed this delightful spot, an easy path leads down through woodland back to the start. The outward leg is through an attractive mixture of both deciduous and coniferous woodland. On a warm day the scent of the pines adds to a memorable walk and the excellent views demand you choose a clear day.

Acres Down Farm specialises in what it does best – cream teas and delicious cakes. No lunches are served but the cream teas are so lavish they are meals in themselves, washed down with tea from a capacious pot. There is an extensive garden and also indoor accommodation. It is open all day from 1st April or Easter, whichever is earlier, until the end of September. Telephone: 02380 813693.

There is no other source of refreshment on this walk.

DISTANCE: 4 miles.

MAP: OS Outdoor Leisure 22 New Forest.

STARTING POINT: Millyford Bridge car park (GR 268078).

HOW TO GET THERE: From the A35 Lyndhurst to Christchurch road half a mile west of Lyndhurst take a minor road signed 'Emery Down'. In the village, turn left immediately after the New Forest Inn, signed 'Bolderwood 3', for a mile and a quarter to Millyford Bridge car park on the right.

ALTERNATIVE STARTING POINT: If you wish to visit the teashop at the beginning or end of your walk, start at Acres Down car park. The teashop is just where the track becomes a surfaced lane. You will then start the walk at point 6.

THE WALK

1. Return towards the road and turn right parallel with the road across a grassy area. When you reach a wooden barrier on the right, cross the road to the Portuguese Fireplace. Take a path from the back

The Portuguese Fireplace

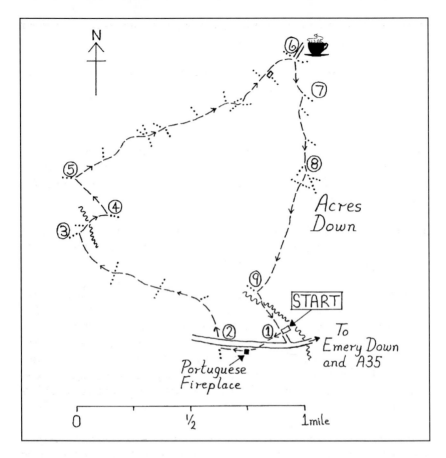

of the memorial and continue in the same direction parallel with the road for 170 yards to a track.

It is rather unexpected to come across a fireplace in the Forest. It is a memorial to Portuguese troops stationed here during the First World War when this structure was the fireplace of their cookhouse, surrounded by huts and tramlines. Wood to shore up trenches was an important material of war and the soldiers worked as lumberjacks. Following difficulties with supply during World War I the Forestry Commission was set up in 1919 to create a strategic reserve of timber.

2. Turn right, cross the road and pass between low wooden posts onto a grassy ride. Go ahead to a small wooden gate then follow a much more defined path for about a quarter of a mile to a track junction. Press on in the same direction, now walking on a clear track, to a T-junction with a cross track.

3. Turn right. Cross a footbridge over Highland Water and continue for 200 yards, uphill, to a track on the left.

4. Turn left.

5. At a T-junction with a cross track turn right. Follow this track for about a mile, ignoring all side turns. Continue past Acres Down car park to Acres Down Farm and tea, on the right just where the track becomes a surfaced lane.

6. Turn left out of the tea garden and return along the lane for 40 yards. At a turning circle take the second of two paths on the left, climbing gently up a sunken track.

7. Just after the track levels out bear right off the main track and pass a wooden barrier after 45 yards. When the path forks after a further 115 yards bear right. The path reaches a second fork after another 175 yards; take the right option again. This brings you out onto the flat expanse of Acres Down where there is a maze of paths large and small. The right route can easily be missed. Keep ahead and watch for a small fenced enclosure a hundred yards or so away on the left.

Though Acres Down is not the highest point in the New Forest, the view is breathtaking, particularly to the south and west. On a clear day it is worth going about 300 yards further on as far as the edge of the plateau for the very best viewpoint. The high ground in the distance is the Isle of Wight. It doesn't look like an island because The Solent is not visible but if you look carefully, you can see the cliffs at the west end. The higher ground in the middle distance is Holmsley Ridge, explored on Walk 5.

8. Level with the far end of the enclosure look for a path branching right. Ignore this and continue for 30 yards to a fork. Bear right. (The left fork takes you to the edge of the plateau.) This path soon leads downhill and into woodland after about 200 yards. Continue down through the trees to a track.

9. Turn left back to the car park where this walk started.

Walk 4
LYNDHURST

If you have time for only one walk in the New Forest, this is the one I would recommend! It visits all the types of scenery for which the Forest is justifiably famous and also has some excellent views. The first couple of miles is through woodland and it is interesting to see the different types, each representing a different aspect of the Forest's history and management. The route starts on a footpath which can be muddy, so be warned, and then joins a well-constructed track. The final mile into Lyndhurst visits the other main type of vegetation, heathery heath, taking a path along a ridge with extensive views in all directions. After visiting the historic capital of the New Forest for tea, the last leg is again through woodland with the final stretch on a particularly attractive path.

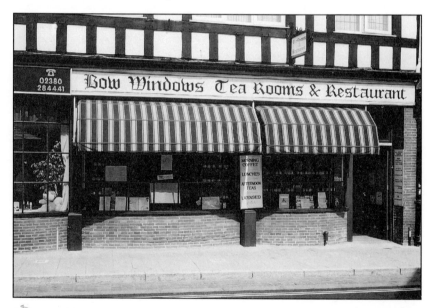

As befits the capital of the New Forest, Lyndhurst has a diverse range of places to eat. The Bow Windows Tea Rooms is a traditional establishment offering traditional fare. Afternoon tea is served all day and includes home-made cakes and scones with clotted cream. There is a wide choice for a light lunch including sandwiches and things on toast as well as a selection of full meals including fish and chips and roasts. Bow Windows are particularly welcoming of children with a special menu that can be coloured in, and high chairs are provided. They are open throughout the year except Mondays from 10 am until 5 pm in summer and 4 pm in winter. Telephone: 02380 282463.

DISTANCE: 5¹/₂ miles.
MAP: OS Landranger 196 Solent and The Isle of Wight.
STARTING POINT: Clayhill Heath car park (GR 302061).
HOW TO GET THERE: The car park where this walk starts is on the A337, the Lyndhurst to Brockenhurst road, about 1 mile south of Lyndhurst.
ALTERNATIVE STARTING POINT: If you wish to visit the teashop at the beginning or end of your walk, start in Lyndhurst where there is ample parking in the main car park. The teashop is on the main street, just by the entrance to the car park. You will then start the walk at point 8.

THE WALK
1. From the far end of the car park, take a broad, grassy path with a bank and fence on the left.

2. When the fence bends sharp left, make your way along the left-hand side of an open area, soon bearing left through a low bank to a gate into an inclosure. Through the gate, the path ahead is much more obvious on the ground. When the main path bends right about 300 yards after the gate, continue ahead to a gravelled track.

3. Turn right.

Over the area covered by this walk the underlying geology and climate remain much the same and yet the exact nature of woodland varies from place to place and the route later traverses an expanse of heathland. These differences reflect various stages in the management of the Forest (see walk 7).

4. When the main track bends right, turn left, soon heading gently uphill, and stay on this track, ignoring all tracks and paths to right and left. Continue ahead when, after about a mile, the main track bears right. The track then narrows to a path leading down to gate and a wooden bridge. Keep on through another gate to a further one that marks the edge of the enclosure.

21

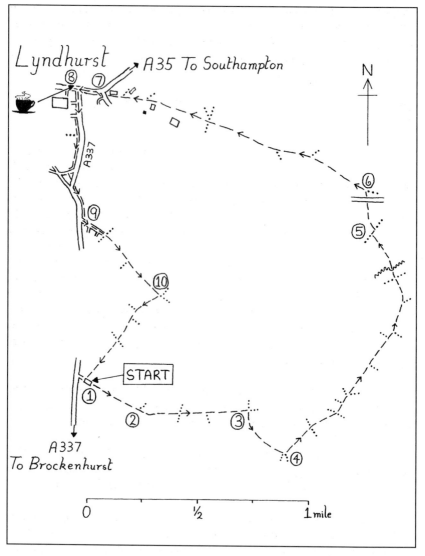

5. Turn right for 40 yards then left to a road. Cross the road and carry on in the same direction for about 50 yards to a clear cross path.

6. Turn left and follow the well-trodden path, which eventually becomes a surfaced track, and continue past the attractive thatched cricket pavilion to a road.

There are extensive views from this ridge across the heath, which is at its best in late summer when the heather is in bloom (see walk 5). This area is called Bolton's Bench after Lord Bolton, Lord Warden of the Forest in 1688. The Lord Warden was the chief officer of the Forest and his underlings supervised everything to do with deer and game. The office was allowed to lapse in the 19th century.

🍵 **7.** Turn right and then left to walk up the High Street to the teashop on the right.

Lyndhurst has long been, and remains, the most important settlement in the New Forest though its appearance is mainly Victorian and Edwardian and its traffic congestion decidedly modern. William I made it the administrative centre of his Nova Foresta and the ancient Court of Verderers still sits here. The name comes from the Norman word 'vert', meaning green, and they originated as officials of the crown administering the cruel and oppressive forest law. Today they are chosen on a more democratic basis and are concerned with the administration of common rights. The court meets six times a year, in public, at the Verderer's Hall in Queen's House. This contains an enormous stirrup, which it is said was used to test whether a dog was large enough to be a danger to deer. If it could not pass through the stirrup it was expedited or 'lawed' - claws were cut from its forefeet so it could not bring down a deer. In the time of Henry III this barbarous practice replaced the even worse one of hamstringing dogs. Though often called King Rufus's Stirrup, in reality it is probably Tudor.

8. Return down the High Street and turn right along Gosport Lane, opposite the Mailmans Arms, signed for Lymington and Brockenhurst. When the road forks at Goose Green, bear left.

9. Take the first road on the left, Beechen Lane. At the end of the road, go through a gate ahead onto a track and continue in the same direction for a good 1/4 mile to the second gate on the right.

10. Turn right through the gate on a clear path with a sign forbidding cycling. When the main path turns right, continue in the same direction on a grassy path. Follow this, ignoring all side turns, back to the start.

Walk 5
HOLMSLEY RIDGE and BURLEY

To those not familiar with the area, New Forest walks sound as if they should be routes through woodland. In fact, the New Forest has extensive areas of heath and this walk explores one of the most scenic. It is an airy circuit through heather with a sense of remote wilderness rare in central southern England. A trifle more energetic than other walks in the New Forest, any exertions are amply rewarded by extensive views.

 Manor Farm Tea Rooms is a charming and traditional establishment situated in a 16th-century thatched building which has been a tea rooms since 1904! For lunch both full meals, such as omelettes or ham and chips, supplemented by daily specials and rounded off by delicious traditional puddings, and lighter snacks are served. On Sunday a full traditional three course lunch is available. There is an excellent range of tempting cakes and a separate menu of inviting ice cream confections. Attached to the tea rooms is a shop selling speciality jams, chutneys and so on. Open throughout the year between 10 am and 5 pm every day except Monday in winter and Monday morning in summer. Telephone: 01425 402218.

DISTANCE: 4¹/₂ miles.
MAP: OS Landranger 195 Bournemouth and Purbeck.
STARTING POINT: Holmsley car park (GR 222012).
HOW TO GET THERE: From the A35 Christchurch to Lyndhurst road 400 yards north of the junction with the B3058, turn off north-west on a minor unsigned road to a car park 1 mile on the right.
ALTERNATIVE STARTING POINT: If you wish to visit the teashop at the beginning or end of your walk, start in Burley where there is ample parking in the village car park. The teashop is on the main street, to the right. You will then start the walk at point 8, taking an unsigned path opposite the newsagent's to reach the junction of gravel tracks described.

THE WALK

1. Return to the road and take a gravelled track almost opposite.

2. When the track bends left, continue ahead on a clear path, passing to the right of a fenced quarry.

When William the Conqueror set aside the New Forest as a private deer hunting preserve in 1079 (see walk 7), it was not uninterrupted woodland. Most of it was heathland and the wooded areas were less extensive than they are today. The wooded inclosures were created by the demand for timber, especially for shipbuilding; the first inclosure act was passed in 1482 and others followed. The idea was to exclude grazing animals and so give the trees a chance to become established.

3. When the path divides take the right fork and follow it down from the ridge and as it skirts to the left of two ponds, Whitten Pond.

During the summer the pond is a picture, with white waterlilies on the water and set in smooth green lawn with gorse bushes around. Yellow, pea-like flowers may be found on the gorse in any month - remember the old saying 'kissing's in season when gorse is in bloom' - but the flowering is at its most profuse in April most years. The pods dry and burst mainly in July. If you sit quietly by a bush on a dry day, you may be able to hear the crackling noise as the pods burst and fling their hard, brown, shiny seeds out. Ants are important for distributing these further afield. They tear and bite at a fleshy orange appendage of the seed, called a caruncle, dragging the seeds along the ground as they do so. A different plant, petty whin, looks like a

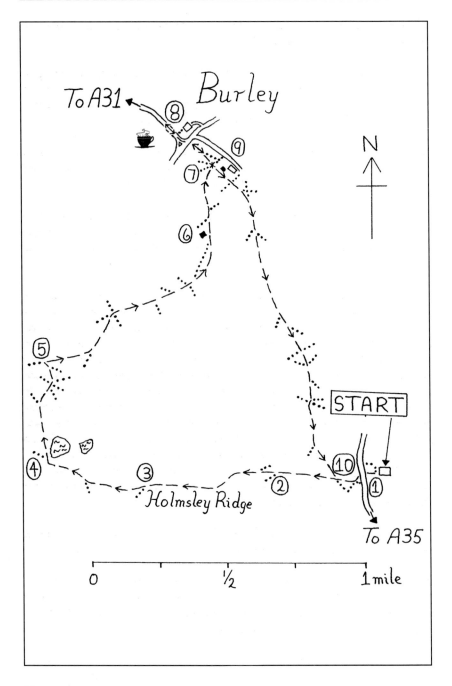

dwarf gorse with tiny, oval leaves. Whin is an old name for gorse and petty is a corruption of petite, meaning small.

4. After passing the ponds turn right. When the path forks bear right. Cross a very wide track - the line of a disused railway - then immediately bear left on a smaller path. At a junction with a larger path turn left for 30 yards to a second major path.

The railway was the Dorchester to Southampton line which was called 'Castleman's Corkscrew' because of its winding route via Brockenhurst, Ringwood and Wimbourne. It opened in 1847 and the last trains ran in 1964.

5. Turn right. Continue uphill as a path joins from the right and then follow the main path, ignoring all turns to both left and right. Soon the path descends into a small valley and joins a surfaced track by a pair of cottages.

The heathlands are at their most attractive in summer when the heather is in bloom. There are actually three species present. In the driest spots bell heather is found. This has a bronze tinge to the leaves which curl over slightly and the flowers, which appear from the end of June onwards, are a deep red-purple. In the wetter areas cross-leaved heath grows. It has larger, pink flowers, also from June onwards, and the whole plant has a somewhat grey look because it is downy. Ling or Scottish heather is by far the commonest of the three with pinkish-purple flowers from July onwards. Often, despite what the botany books say, all three species can be found growing together. Other plants are found among the heather including heath milkwort with dark blue or pink flowers, tormentil with four-petalled yellow flowers and lousewort with hooded pink blooms from April to July. Dodder is a parasitic plant which may be found on heather, gorse and other plants. It does not make its own food but absorbs it from the host plant by suckers arising from reddish-brown threads. It has pale pink flowers between July and September.

6. Follow the track to a surfaced drive and turn right to where it finishes at a junction of gravelled tracks. Note this point (*).

7. Take none of the tracks but go ahead into a wooded area to pick up a path bearing slightly left. Follow it through the trees and downhill to emerge on the road in Burley. Turn left and follow the main road round to the teashop on the left.

Smuggling, or free-trading as it was often called, was a national pastime in the first part of the 19th century, encouraged by high prices and swingeing taxes. Not just the criminal fraternity but whole communities were involved, with the necessary capital provided by the squire, doctor and parson. The south coast of Hampshire was ideally suited with creeks and inlets giving easy access to the cover of the Forest. The Queen's Head in Burley was one of the smugglers' headquarters though today it is better known for its associations with hunting. A small force of Riding Officers, to chase smugglers on land, and Revenue Cutters, to pursue them at sea, were employed by Customs and Excise but were not very successful; the smugglers' boats could outrun the cutters at sea and on land the community was organised to warn of the coming of the Riding Officers. One young woman, Lovey Warne, from near Burley used to stand on Vereley Hill, just north of the village, wearing a bright red cloak whenever danger threatened.

8. After tea retrace your steps through the village and wood to the junction of gravel tracks (*).

9. Now continue ahead, passing to the right of a wooden building, public conveniences, and a car park. Take a gravelled path ahead and follow this out along the top of the hill then down into a valley, crossing the disused railway again at a demolished bridge, and up the other side to the track followed near the start.

10. Turn left, back to the start.

Walk 6
WILVERLEY INCLOSURE

*W*ater *is always a great attraction and this walk starts at a popular picnic spot beside Avon Water. The route described here climbs to Wilverley Plain with the famous Naked Man, now sadly enfeebled but still a reminder of the brutal fate awaiting those convicted of robbery or smuggling in the past. The next section is charming woodland walking through Wilverley Inclosure to the teashop before returning by Avon Water.*

The Old Station Tea Rooms are in the disused Holmsley Station. When the line closed in 1964, the station lay empty for several years before it was refurbished and reopened as a popular tea rooms and it reflects its history in its decoration. There are tables outside on what was the station forecourt, now edged with an attractive garden. Various set teas also echo its history, such as the Stationmaster's Tea with sandwiches and cake or the plainer Porter's Tea with just bread and butter and cake. Cream teas include clotted cream. Lunches are served between 12 noon and 1.30 pm and include both full meals and lighter alternatives such as sandwiches and ploughman's. The Old Station Tea Rooms are open every day except Monday (open Bank Holiday Mondays) throughout the year except in January and February when they open at weekends only. In summer they are open between 10 am and 5.30 pm, closing half an hour earlier in winter. Telephone: 01425 402468.

When the teashop is closed, there is no other source of refreshment on this walk.

DISTANCE: 4¹/₂ miles.
MAP: OS Landranger 195 Bournemouth and Purbeck.
STARTING POINT: Wootton Bridge car park (GR 251996).
HOW TO GET THERE: Directions are given from the A35 Lyndhurst to Christchurch road. Some 6 miles south-west of Lyndhurst there is a complex junction where coming from either north or south you have to turn left off the main road, signed 'Burley and Setthorns caravan site', there being no right turn from either direction. Having left the A35, turn right at a T junction, towards Brockenhurst. After about a mile, just after crossing a cattle grid, turn right to Wootton Bridge car park, on the right just before the bridge.
ALTERNATIVE STARTING POINT: If you wish to visit the teashop at the beginning or end of your walk, start at Osmonds Bushes car park near the junction on the A35 described above. The teashop is across the main road and along the road opposite. You will then start the walk at point 8 if you visit the teashop first or 9 if you decide to visit it last.

THE WALK

1. With your back to the entrance to the car park, go to the right-hand side of the car park and go uphill, threading between the gorse bushes, bearing right to walk parallel with the lane on the right. A road sign soon comes into view and you head for this.

2. At a road junction cross the road and take a broad, grassy path opposite, still climbing parallel with the road. Cross the track to Wilverley Inclosure car park and continue to a surfaced drive to a second car park, Wilverley Plain.

Wilverley Plain was ploughed up during the dark days of the Second World War when there was a real fear of food shortages. The fences were removed and the area reseeded in 1952.

3. Turn left. Walk to the end of the car park and continue along the

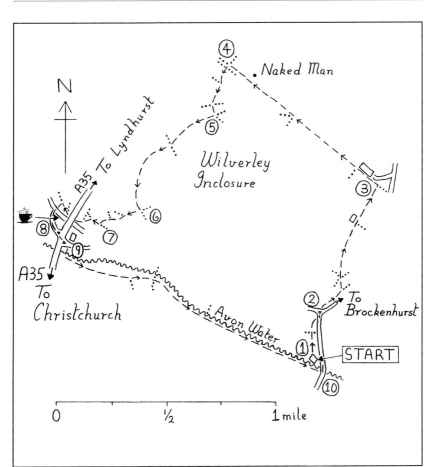

track ahead for ½ mile. Watch for the fenced stump of the Naked Man on the right.

This was once a great oak tree whose thick boughs were used as a gallows to hang some of the New Forest's highwaymen and smugglers. The name first appears on maps in the 18th century when the tree may have resembled a giant naked figure.

4. Some 130 yards after the Naked Man turn left through a field gate. Follow the path ahead, walking along the edge of some conifers on the left. When the conifers end, continue ahead over a cross path to a second cross path.

Wilverley, one of the largest inclosures in the Forest, was first inclosed in 1775 but the original planting failed and it was replanted in 1809 with oak and some of the trees on the edge near the car park date from that time. It was opened in 1846 and fenced again 50 years later when many of the oaks were felled and replaced with conifers. Some of this planting has now reached maturity and felled in turn with new planting of Corsican pine. The reason so much of the planting in more recent times has been of conifers is that these are very quick growing in the warm(!), wet British climate on the poor soils typically used for forestry. One of the reasons the New Forest has survived over 900 years despite the political and economic changes down the centuries is that its soils are poor and are not attractive for agriculture.

5. Turn right. Continue across a track and walk along the path for just under ¹⁄₂ mile as it curves left down an attractive small valley.

6. Turn right at a cross path, uphill out of the valley. At the top of the rise bear left on a larger path to a gate.

7. Immediately through the gate, turn right on a cross path. When the fence on the right soon ends, bear left. Follow the path down under a bridge and stay on it, ignoring all paths on the right, as far as some overhead wires. At this point turn left along a grassy ride to a stile. Go ahead a few yards to a road and the teashop.

Holmsley Station was originally called Christchurch Road and was the end of the line. Passengers alighted here and were taken by horse drawn carriage to the popular resorts of Christchurch and Bournemouth. It had many famous visitors including Edward VII and his mistress Lillie Langtry, and Kaiser Wilhelm.

8. Turn left from the teashop along a road to the A35. Cross the busy main road and continue along the road opposite for a few yards.

9. Opposite the entrance to Osmonds Bushes car park turn right to a stile. Walk ahead to a bridge over the river then turn left. The path lies between the inclosure fence on the right and the river on the left. At first the path veers away from the river and is nearer the fence but then returns to the river bank. This stretch can be muddy and a little rough in places though the path is perfectly clear and easy to follow. Continue on the path for about a mile to a lane.

10. Turn left over a bridge, back to the start.

Walk 7
QUEEN BOWER and BROCKENHURST

The New Forest is a mosaic of habitats and this route is very varied with both heath and woodland walking. The highlight is the superb oaks at Queen Bower, which show just how lush the Forest can be. A very easy ramble with almost no climbing, this walk is highly recommended.

 The Brock and Bruin Tea Room on Brookley Road in Brockenhurst is a bustling traditional teashop in a modern building. The theme suggested by the name is well maintained with teddy bears of all shapes and sizes watching you scoff your cakes. There is an excellent choice of delicious cakes and other teatime goodies including cream teas with clotted cream. Lunch is served between 11.30 am and 2.30 pm and choices include deep fried vegetables with a dip and stuffed pancakes as well as sandwiches, baguettes and jacket potatoes. This is a particularly refreshing stop available all year (except for two weeks between Christmas and New Year) between 9.30 am and 5.30 pm. Telephone: 01590 622020.

DISTANCE: 5 miles.

MAPS: OS Landranger 195 Bournemouth and Purbeck, with the Brockenhurst section of the walk on 196 The Solent and The Isle of Wight.

STARTING POINT: Beachern Wood car park (GR 284026).

HOW TO GET THERE: Follow the signs for Rhinefield from the A337 at Brockenhurst to Beachern Wood car park on the right, just after the 40mph sign. Alternatively, take a minor road signed 'Rhinefield' from the A35 Christchurch to Lyndhurst road, in which case the car park is on the left just before the outskirts of Brockenhurst. This latter route takes you through the famous Rhinefield ornamental drive. Mature specimen trees line the road. They were mostly planted around 1859 and several are the tallest of their species in Britain.

ALTERNATIVE STARTING POINT: If you wish to visit the teashop at the beginning or end of your walk, start in Brockenhurst where there is ample parking in the village car park (note this has a 4 hour maximum stay except on Sundays and bank holidays). The teashop is across the road to the right. You will then start the walk at point 11.

THE WALK

1. Walk along the lawn parallel with the lane passing the car park. When the lane bends right, take a clear path forking left. Join a path coming in from the left and continue ahead to a footbridge.

Ober Water is a typical New Forest stream with water tinged red-brown. This is caused by the rainwater draining through peaty soil and picking up iron and other minerals.

2. Cross the bridge. Turn right and then left after 20 yards, forking right almost immediately.

3. Turn right at a T junction with a cross path then left by a cottage. When the track ends, turn right on an ill-defined path, walking with a stream, sometimes dry, on the right. After joining another stream, which the path crosses, the stream bears right, away from the path. Continue in the same direction across heath on a now rather more defined path.

4. Cross a footbridge and follow the path into a wooded area. After crossing another footbridge, bear right on the main path and bear right again when the track forks and follow it across heathland.

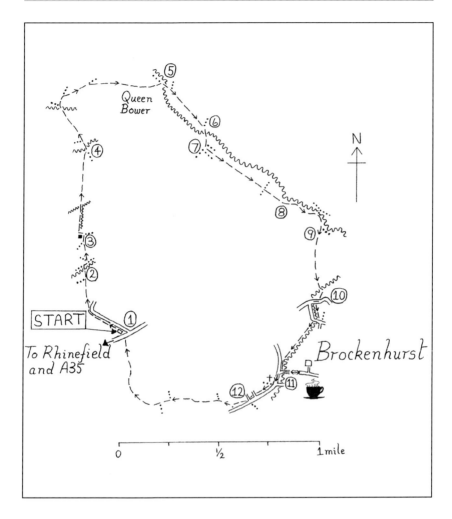

When a plantation on the left ends, bear right again rather than left into a Wildlife Conservation Area.

5. At a river turn right to yet another footbridge. Cross the bridge where there is a welcome seat to admire the ancient trees. Follow the path ahead.

Queen Bower is one of the most attractive spots in the Forest with a stream winding through old oaks. It is said that this was the favourite walk of a queen but whether it

35

was Philippa, wife of Edward III, or Eleanor, Edward I's consort, depends on which authority you consult.

6. At a T junction with a track, with a gate immediately to the left, turn right to a further footbridge, somewhat larger than those encountered previously.

7. Some 85 yards after crossing the bridge, just before the wood on the left ends, turn left on a clear path through the trees.

Deer may be seen around here, or indeed almost anywhere in the New Forest. They are the reason for the Forest's existence. William the Conqueror was an enthusiastic huntsman and in or about 1079 he set aside this region, which he named the New Forest, for the preservation of the deer for his sport. The hated forest law was added to the normal laws of the land forbidding the felling of trees, protection of farmland from deer, grazing animals when they might interfere with the well-being of the deer, keeping a dog and, above all, killing deer. These laws were enforced with extreme severity. As time went on, royalty were less interested in hunting and the importance of the Forest for other purposes became more important so the management evolved. Nonetheless, there are some 1,500 deer of five species to be found in the Forest and the number is kept at this level by culling to maintain a healthy population that does not interfere with other activities. Noisy walkers with dogs are most unlikely to catch a glimpse of these elusive animals - they will see and hear you long before you see them!

Eventually, the forest became more important as a source of timber for ships, especially in view of its proximity to the important south coast ports. Until the middle of the 18th century, the woods and timber inclosures consisted of native hardwoods such as oak and beech but from the 1770s faster growing, softwood coniferous trees were introduced. The pine woods are not so rich in wildlife: an oak wood will support some 4,000 species whereas coniferous forest has perhaps a quarter of that. Some of the oldest inclosures have become part of the open forest and are classified under the portentous title of Ancient and Ornamental Woodlands. These extend to about 8,000 acres while inclosures, both hardwood and softwood, are about 22,000 acres. This diversity of habitat has led to a great variety of wildlife. For example, 29 out of the 39 British species of dragonfly are found in the New Forest.

8. When the path approaches a river, pick up a good path on its right bank, soon passing a footbridge, which the route does not cross. About 100 yards after passing the bridge, the main path bears right away from the river. Follow it across a small footbridge and out of the wood.

9. Walk towards Brockenhurst, seen ahead. After crossing another small footbridge, bear half left to a further bridge to emerge on the road opposite the Cloud Hotel, a large cream building.

This is Butts Lawn. The New Forest lawns are maintained by the grazing of livestock. There are about 3,000 ponies as well as cattle, pigs, donkeys and even geese. All these animals are owned by Forest commoners who have the right to turn out stock to graze. These rights date back to the time when fencing the Forest was forbidden because it would interfere with the free movement of the king's deer and they are administered by the Court of Verderers. Today this consists of five members appointed by the various official bodies concerned with the Forest and five representatives elected by the commoners. (See also walk 4.)

10. Turn right. Just before crossing the river, next to Pine Cottage, turn left on a path along the river bank. Cross the river at a ford and footbridge and continue by the river on a signed footpath. When the path joins a road, continue in the same direction to Brookley Road, the main street of Brockenhurst, on the left. Turn up this and the teashop is on the right.

Brockenhurst is one of the principal settlements of the New Forest and its ancient church is mentioned in the Domesday Book. It has expanded considerably in both size and importance since the coming of the railway in 1849.

11. After tea return to the ford and turn left. Opposite the church, cross the road to a footpath by the right-hand side of the road.

This is not the ancient church referred to above which lies some way to the east of the modern village but a more modern foundation built in 1903. Much of the planned carving was never finished so it lacks the intended Gothic flourishes.

12. Just after Armstrong Lane bear right away from the road on a track. Turn right at a cross track, signed 'North Weirs' at the road. Stay on the main track and follow it to the road almost opposite the car park.

Walk 8
MILFORD-on-SEA

The two parts of this delightful walk are in complete contrast. The outward leg follows a breezy clifftop path with views of the Isle of Wight. This is always interesting, with a multitude of craft from sailing dinghies to ocean going liners in the Solent. The route then cuts inland to the attractive village centre of Milford-on-Sea for tea before returning to the start by quiet woodland paths beside the pretty Dane's Stream.

 Polly's Pantry Tea Rooms is a friendly, welcoming, traditional tea room behind a cake shop on the High Street in Milford-on-Sea. You choose a cake to enjoy with your tea from the range on display in the shop and clotted cream teas are also served. For a light lunch sandwiches are available as well as omelettes, salads or ploughman's. They are open throughout the year between 8.30 am and 5 pm every day except Sunday. Telephone: 01590 645558.

When the teashop is closed, there are several pubs in Milford-on-Sea, notably the Smugglers Inn, passed on the route, which serves food and has a garden.

DISTANCE: 3 miles.
MAPS: OS Landranger 195 Bournemouth and Purbeck, with the easternmost section of the walk on 196 Solent and The Isle of Wight.
STARTING POINT: Most westerly of the sea front car parks at Milford-on-Sea (GR 276918).
HOW TO GET THERE: Take the B3058 Milford-on-Sea to Christchurch road to the western edge of Milford-on-Sea.
ALTERNATIVE STARTING POINT: If you wish to visit the teashop at the beginning or end of your walk, start in the centre of Milford-on-Sea, parking in the village car park in Sea Road. You will then start the walk at point 4.

THE WALK

1. From the back of the car park turn left along the cliffs and follow the surfaced path for about a mile.

Milford-on-Sea is at the mouth of the Solent and there are wonderful views of the busy shipping and across to the Isle of Wight with the huge chalk stacks of the Needles rising from the water. The Isle of Wight causes the unusual double tides in the Solent. The last of the flood up the Channel sweeps round the eastern end of the island where it meets the water already ebbing out and drives it back as a second high tide.

2. When the surfaced path ends by the Marine Cafe, walk on the shingle with the sea wall on the right then continue ahead on a shingle bank.

Hurst Castle, seen ahead, was built by Henry VIII at the end of this shingle spit, $1^{1}/_{2}$ miles away. It was one of a series of coastal defences built to guard against attack by the French and Spanish. It has also been used as a prison. Charles I was briefly kept here on his way from Carisbrooke Castle on the Isle of Wight to trial in London. The castle is said to be haunted by another prisoner, a Roman Catholic priest, Paul Atkinson, who was incarcerated in 1700 during a clampdown on Roman Catholicism and remained there until his death 30 years later. Hurst Castle is no relic from Tudor times. It was substantially strengthened during the Napoleonic War and fortified with anti-aircraft and searchlight batteries during the Second World War. The last troops left in 1945 and it is now open to the public every day in

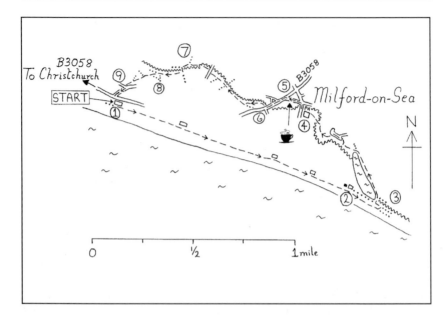

the summer. You can get there by walking along this shingle bank or by ferry from Keyhaven. Telephone: 01425 610784.

3. Take the first path down on the left to a track. Turn left for 60 yards then turn right across a footbridge. Follow the path ahead with a tidal pool on the left and ignore paths to the right. At the end of the gravelled path, go up some steps on the right to a road. Walk along the pavement for about 100 yards then bear left to continue on a gravel path to a car park.

4. Go to the far right-hand corner of the car park and turn right along a road. At a junction turn left to the teashop on the left.

Milford-on-Sea dates back to at least Saxon times and was mentioned in the Domesday Book, though it has grown from the four families with six slaves, a mill and a church described in that survey. The village green is a remnant of a once more extensive area of commons and the peaceful and attractive centre is designated a conservation area. It is difficult to imagine that this law abiding community was once the centre of a pitched battle with the law enforcement agencies but that is what happened in the 18th century when smugglers battled with excise men and militia on the green. Milford's connections with 'free-trading' are recognised in the Smugglers Inn, previously called The Crown.

5. From the teashop turn left then left again at a road junction.

6. Immediately after a bridge over a river, turn right on a path along the river bank. Ignore all side paths and cross a road to continue by the river, soon crossing it at a footbridge to walk with the river on your left.

In the 1880s a local landowner, Colonel Cornwallis-West, had visions of turning Milford into a seaside resort to rival Eastbourne and Bournemouth and so the '-on-Sea' was added to the village's name. His grand schemes came to nothing but he did give this land bordering the Dane's Stream to the community to be used as Pleasure Grounds.

7. At a T junction with a cross path, turn left then, after 30 yards and by a seat, bear left to recross the river. Immediately after the footbridge, turn right to continue by the river for about 200 yards.

8. Ignore a path on the left then bear left at a fork after a further 15 yards. Continue ahead as a path soon joins on the left then bear left at a fork after a further 50 yards. Follow the path through to a road.

9. Cross over to a second road and turn right, back to the start.

Walk 9
LEPE and EXBURY

This walk is the most varied of those described in this book and a microcosm of much that Hampshire has to offer. It encompasses quiet field paths and woodland and a particularly interesting stretch of coast with unrivalled views of the Isle of Wight and the busy shipping in the Solent. Tea is at Exbury Gardens, at their glorious best in spring and autumn. In summer you might choose to spend some time on the beach at Lepe, a popular spot for sunbathing and swimming.

 The tea rooms at Exbury Gardens are part of the original forge of the estate, attractively decorated and with a woodburning stove, lit in the cooler months. There are also tables outside. A good range of cakes and biscuits is on offer with clotted cream teas. For lunch, served between noon and 3 pm, there are sandwiches and soup or filled jacket potatoes and a daily selection of specials. Between mid February and the end of October the tea rooms are open every day from 10 am until 5.30 pm. Telephone: 02380 898737.

When the tea rooms are closed, there is no other source of refreshment on the route. Some 600 yards off the route, however, you will find the restaurant at Lepe, which remains open at weekends in winter. Telephone: 01703 893681. To reach it turn left along the road at point 7.

DISTANCE: 6 miles
MAP: OS Landranger 196 Solent and The Isle of Wight.
STARTING POINT: Dark Water car park (GR 433013).
HOW TO GET THERE: From the A326, the Southampton to Fawley road, at a roundabout west of Fawley, take a minor road signed for the Gang Warily Centre, Blackfield and Lepe. Continue over the first crossroads. At the crossroads by the Hampshire Yeoman, turn right along Exbury Road, signed 'Exbury 2', to a car park on the right.
ALTERNATIVE STARTING POINT: If you wish to visit the teashop at the beginning or end of your walk, start at Exbury Gardens where there is a large car park, though permission should be sought before leaving a car for a long period. You will then start the walk at point 13.

THE WALK

1. Continue south along the lane for about ½ mile, down into a dip and up the other side, passing paths on the left and right.

2. When the road bends sharp right, turn left on a footpath along a track for 200 yards.

3. Just before the track bends left, turn right on a path along the left hand side of a field, way-marked by yellow arrows on a post. At the end of the field continue in the same direction on a path through woodland to a metal gate and onto a track. Turn right for 25 yards to a second, larger track.

4. Turn left along the track to a farm then continue on the signed bridleway into a field, turning right to follow a hedge on the right.

5. At the end of the field turn right for 15 yards then right again along a signed footpath. Follow this over a footbridge and ahead into and across a field and a narrow strip. At the time of writing, the path had not been well reinstated across the next field but it skirts a copse on the left and goes to a stile about 100 yards to the left of a further wood on the right. In the next field continue ahead to a stile by a

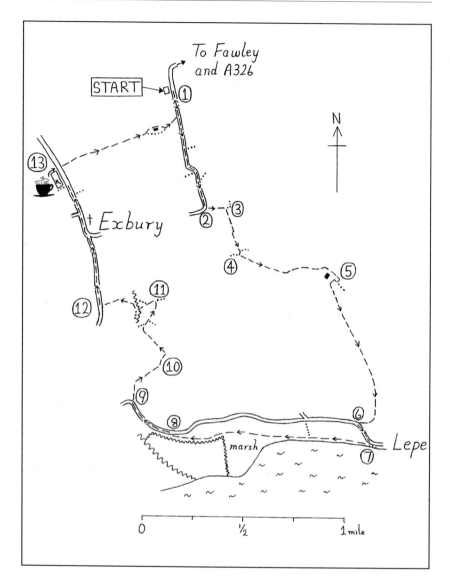

field gate. Cross the next field and in the field after that bear right to a stile by a gate onto a lane.

6. Turn left along the lane.

Lepe has had several spellings down the centuries. The name could be used on the television programme 'Call My Bluff' as there are three theories: one says it comes from a legendary causeway to the Isle of Wight, which had a gap you had to leap, a second suggests it derives from an Anglo-Saxon word for a type of basket and the third holds that it originated from the Roman word for stone, 'lapis'. There has been a port here since Roman times and by the 16th century it was a prosperous fishing village with two harbours, one at Lepe village and a second just east at Stone Point. The latter was destroyed when thousands of tons of shingle were thrown up in a great storm in 1703. The remaining harbour silted up by 1825. In more recent times Mulberry Harbours, used in the D-Day invasion, were assembled here. Over 6,000 troops and 2,000 vehicles were despatched for the invasion in June 1944. They and their ammunition collected in this area, which was cordoned off during the build up.

7. When the lane reaches the coast, turn right on a signed path along the shore. When the constructed path finishes, continue along the shingle and then over a more grassy path, in the same direction but now further away from the shore, to a lane. (Note: the shore path can be covered at the highest tides. Therefore, check the tide times when planning this walk or turn right at point 6 and walk along the lane to rejoin the route at point 8. Alternatively, there is a path up from the shore to the lane connecting points 6 and 8.)

This area of the Solent coast has been protected from development and is now a country park. The wooden groynes are there to break the force of the sea and protect the land. Notice how they have been covered by brown algae. These evolved to live on rocky shores but have been able to colonise this habitat provided by human activity. They photosynthesize when covered by the sea and are brown because they have extra pigments to make the best use of the light available under water. There are several species, adapted to tolerate different amounts of exposure to air. The mud flats are a Site of Special Scientific Interest. These are not particularly attractive to the human eye but are very rich biologically. The mud is home to enormous quantities of small animals, which are food for all sorts of wading birds.

8. Turn left along the lane.

9. When the lane bends left, cross a grassy area on the right to a wooden kissing gate onto a path through a belt of trees. Follow the path round to the right, as shown by a finger post, and go down into a dip, across a plank bridge, up the other side then over another plank bridge into a field.

10. Turn left and walk to a finger post. At this point, turn left again, as shown by the sign, and walk with a hedge on the left. At the end of the field, continue round the edge to the right to pick up a faint track and follow it along the left-hand side of the next field then round to the left.

11. Turn left along a clear track into a wood, signed by a finger post. When the track bears right into a field, continue ahead on a path in the wood. Just after a plank bridge over a stream, turn right, as indicated by a yellow arrow on a post but 10 yards after the post! Follow the path through the wood and across a field to a lane.

12. Turn right along the lane. At a road junction carry on in the same direction, signed 'Beaulieu 4', to the teashop at the rear of the car park for Exbury Gardens.

Lionel Rothschild was a banker by profession but a gardener on a prodigious scale by vocation. He created the gardens here from 1919 onwards with astounding energy and resources: 150 men were recruited just to prepare the ground by double digging, adding peat as they went, and this went on for 10 years. These labourers were in addition to the 60 full time gardeners with a further 10 just for the glasshouses. He specialised in rhododendrons, which thrive on the acid soil, rich in ancient leaf mould, and bred many award winning new varieties. The gardens are now mature and the thorough preparation has proved its worth. From the start of spring with the early flowering rhododendrons, magnolias and daffodils through the height of the flowering season in May and June to the wonderful autumn blaze of colour, Exbury is an exceptionally outstanding woodland garden at its peak. It is open every day from the beginning of March to the beginning of November from 10 am until 5.30 pm (or dusk if earlier). Telephone: 01703 899422.

13. Leave the car park at the signed exit. Cross the road and take a track directly opposite. Ignore all side turnings and when the track forks, bear left past farm buildings and continue to a lane. Turn left, back to the start.

Walk 10
HAMBLE

Almost none of this walk is on public footpaths! Fortunately, Hamble Common and Copse are managed by Eastleigh District Council Countryside Service. They have opened up and signed several paths, making possible this short, interesting walk centred round the quaint old heart of the port of Hamble.

The Village Tea Rooms in Hamble serve a good selection of delicious home-made cakes along with cream teas and excellent shortbread. Options for a light lunch include sandwiches and filled jacket potatoes with home-made soup in winter and there are daily specials for a more substantial meal. Opening at the unusually early hour of 7.30 am in the summer (until 6 pm), the full English breakfasts on offer are very popular with the yachting enthusiasts who abound on the Hamble. In winter, between November and Easter, the opening times are from 9 am until 5 pm. The building housing the tea rooms is about 300 years old. Part used to be the premises of a coffin maker and the rest was a rope works; the teapot sign hangs from what was once part of the pulley system. The premises are reputed to be haunted by the ghost of a sailor. Apparently, he had a girl friend in the village. He was returning to his ship when the horse he was riding collapsed and died with the result he was court martialled for being late returning and beheaded. The present owner says she has never seen him but strange things have happened... Telephone: 02380 455583.

DISTANCE: 2½ miles.
MAP: OS Landranger 196 Solent and The Isle of Wight.
STARTING POINT: Hamble village green car park (GR 483066).
HOW TO GET THERE: From junction 8 on the M27, follow the signs for Hamble (the B3397). Continue along the road into the outskirts of the village and turn right along Copse Road, signed for 'Hamble Common, Hamble Point and the Marina'. Take the first turning on the left, School Lane, and then the first right, in fact Green Lane but unsigned at the time of writing, to a car park on the far side of the village green on the right.
ALTERNATIVE STARTING POINT: If you wish to visit the teashop at the beginning or end of your walk, start in the main car park in the centre of Hamble. The teashop is across the road. You will then start the walk at point 7.

THE WALK

1. From the far right-hand corner of the car park, take a path signed 'Hamble Common' by a noticeboard explaining something of the importance of this area. Follow the clear path as it wends its way through woodland to the common.

2. At a kissing gate on the right, follow the path along the shore and then round to the right to a path junction, signed by a finger post.

3. Turn left, signed 'Hamble Point via estuary'. After crossing a footbridge with a wooden handrail, continue ahead on a path beside the estuary, marked with a green arrow. At the fence surrounding Hamble Point Marina, follow the path round to the right, again marked with a green arrow, to a road.

Estuaries such as this support a distinctive community of plants. The soil - or mud - is salty due to occasional inundation by the tide and this makes it difficult for the plants to absorb water by osmosis. Therefore, despite living in a place where there would seem to be plenty of water, the plants can be in a state known as physiological drought and many of them have adaptations to help them conserve

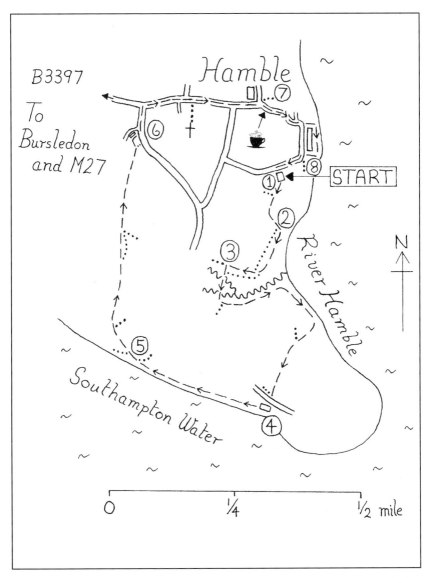

B3397

To
Bursledon
and M27

Hamble

START

N

Southampton Water

River Hamble

0   ¼   ½ mile

the water they do manage to absorb. Typical species seen here include sea purslane, which has small, succulent, rather greyish leaves, and the rather exotic looking glasswort. This is a very succulent, fleshy plant whose cylindrical shoots are made up of obvious segments. The activities of these and other plants slowly transform the salt marsh, adding organic matter as they die and decay and raising the level so it *is covered by the sea less often. This gradual change makes it more suitable for other plants, less tolerant of the extreme conditions, which gradually invade; to the right of the path small oaks are beginning to grow.*

4. Cross the road to a car park and turn right on a path signed 'Hamble Copse via foreshore'.

The Solent is said to be home to the largest pleasure sailing fleet in the world with over 32,000 berths in the many marinas. The Hamble estuary, with over 3,000 of those berths, has been one of the most important for decades thanks to the broad estuary. It seems amazing to me they can all find enough sea to sail on but many apparently rarely leave their berths! Not only is this position ideal for yachting but has also long been of military significance due to its command of Southampton Water. The Bofors Gun from the Second World War is a reminder of this and along this stretch of shore was also a gun emplacement from the Napoleonic War and one of Henry VIII's coastal forts, the latter commanded by a reformed pirate, Sir Henry Maynwaring. This coast has been important for the defence of the realm down the centuries, but it has also been at risk. During the 100 Years War, in 1377 the priory, passed later in the walk, was sacked and burned by the French.

5. Shortly before the BP works, recognizable by the long jetty, join a larger path coming in from the right and follow it as it curves right away from the shore, again following the green arrows. Stay on the main path, soon crossing a grassy glade then continuing through trees. Ignore a path on the right, signed 'Hamble Village', and continue ahead, signed 'Hamble Copse'. Watch out for a carved tree trunk to the right of the path. Bear left at the next finger post to a road.

The oil terminal you have just passed receives oil by pipeline for distribution by tanker.

6. Turn left to a T junction with a main road and turn right into Hamble. At the square with the main village car park on the left, continue on the narrow road ahead and the teashop is on the right.

The church on the right is all that remains of a priory established here from 1109 by monks from Thiron near Chartres and it still retains some features from that time. For example, on each side of the altar is a carved head, one of a novice of the order and one of a bearded monk. The door is covered in knife marks made by local fishermen - a downwards stroke made before departure and a horizontal cut completing the cross in thanksgiving for a safe return. Hamble has a long association with the sea and was a fishing port famous for oysters until the Second World War. In more recent times, apart from pleasure sailing, the aviation industry has been more important. In the church is a memorial to Sir Edwin Alliot Verdon-Roe, the first Englishman to fly. During the First World War he built an aircraft factory on the outskirts of Hamble and the airfield remained in use for training pilots until 1984.

7. From the teashop turn right down the cobbled High Street to the shore. When the road turns right, go ahead along the side of a car park to the edge of the hard. Turn right, passing the ferry to Warsash, then right again at the far end of the car park, passing a plaque summarising the contribution of Hamble to the war effort in the Second World War.

The street winding down the hill to the seashore seems like a bit of Cornwall translated into Hampshire brick. It is lined with numerous old houses, many of them dating back to Georgian times when Hamble was an important shipbuilding centre. This supported various crafts and trades: the street called Rope Walk recalls the rope making that once went on and Copperhill Terrace, a row of 18th-century houses overlooking the square, is named after the coppers in which the tar for preserving the ropes was boiled.

8. Turn left along the road and follow it round to the right, uphill, back to the car park where the walk started.

Walk 11
THE UPPER HAMBLE VALLEY

A delightful area of ancient woodland on the north bank of the Hamble is managed as a country park by Hampshire County Council. This means the footpaths are well maintained and there are ample car parks. Much of this outstanding walk is within the 400 acres of the country park. At its heart is a farm with buildings dating back to the 15th century, which is now an exceptionally lively and interesting museum. A visit is very highly recommended so you need to allow plenty of time for this.

 Manor Farm Pantry Tea Rooms are housed in an attractive modern building at the entrance to the farm, with an extensive patio outside. Excellent cakes, all made on the premises, are served along with sandwiches and daily specials for lunch such as cheese pasta bake with salad and crusty bread. The Pantry is open every day between 10.30 am and 5 pm from Easter to the end of October and on Sundays in winter. Telephone: 01489 787055.

There is no other source of refreshment on this walk.

DISTANCE: 3 miles.

MAP: OS Landranger 196 Solent and The Isle of Wight.

STARTING POINT: Bottom Copse car park, Manor Farm Country Park, Pylands Lane, Bursledon (GR 495111).

HOW TO GET THERE: From the junction of the M27 with the A3024, junction 8, follow the signs eastward to Manor Farm Country Park on Pylands Lane. Entry is free but parking charges apply between Easter and October and are collected on entry. Continue along the entrance road to the fourth small parking area on the right, Bottom Copse.

ALTERNATIVE STARTING POINT: If you wish to visit the teashop at the beginning or end of your walk, start in the car park by the farm, reached by following the entrance road to its far end. You will then start the walk at point 8.

THE WALK

1. Take a footpath, marked by a yellow ringed post, from the rear of the middle section of the car park to a T junction with a cross path. Turn left on this path, parallel with a horse trail, to a T junction with a track, ignoring all cross paths.

2. Turn right, passing immediately a path on the left to toilets and a picnic area. Follow the track first beside a tidal creek and then the river Hamble.

3. Soon after a bench, with a wonderful view up the Hamble, turn right on a stepped path. Do not go onto the shore but continue along the fenced path. Cross another path down from the main track and carry on to a T junction.

The river Hamble is famous for its shipbuilding (see walk 10), from the Grace de Dieu built in 1418 to the yachts of today. The Grace de Dieu was struck by lightning in 1439 and burned. The fittings were saved but not the wreck, which lies on the river bed. Just downstream King Alfred's men are supposed to have sunk 20 Viking longships at the battle of Brixedone. The river has also been an important transport artery with bricks and timber being carried this way.

4. Turn right.

5. At a cross path turn right downhill, cross a small tidal creek then continue up the other side. At the top of the slope, take the centre

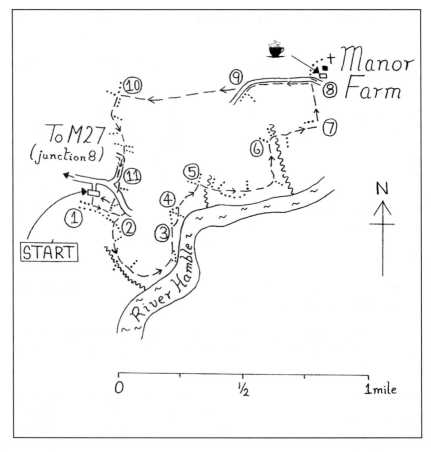

one of three paths. Stay on the clear, main path, ignoring all side paths to left and right.

If you had been able to visit Hampshire 3,000 years ago, after the end of the last Ice Age but before humans had much influence, the landscape would have been very different. The country would almost all have been clothed in mixed deciduous woodland - the temperate rain forest. Human activity has removed it all and today there are few extensive areas of ancient woodland left so those that do remain are very important.

6. When the main path bends sharply left, continue in the same direction on a smaller path. Cross a footbridge and then a stile, which takes you out of the country park. Follow the path through and out of the woodland and along the left-hand side of a field as far as a gate on the left.

☕ **7.** Turn left through the gate onto a track that leads to a road. The teashop is across the road, a few yards right.

At Manor Farm you are invited to step back to the turn of the century to visit a working farm, complete with all the sounds and smells associated with the animals. The whole experience is made more immediate by the characters who inhabit the farmhouse and its adjoining cottage. The farmer's wife, 'Mrs Earwicker', goes about her daily tasks while next door lives the schoolmistress, 'Miss Stubbs', whose bell will summon you for a lesson in the Victorian classroom. Nearby are the blacksmith's forge and wheelwright's shop and the 13th-century church of St Bartholomew. There is a charge for entry to this enjoyable museum, which is open between 10 am and 5 pm every day from Easter to October and on Sundays (except the first and last of the year) in winter. Telephone: 01489 787055.

8. Return to the junction of track and road and take a path to the left of the road and parallel to it.

9. At a gate across the path, go through a gap in the hedge on the right. Cross the road to pick up a track on the other side and walk along this for about 1/2 mile.

10. Immediately after a cross track, that on the left leading to a house called Cricketwood, turn left through a kissing gate on a signed path. Ignore all side paths and continue when it becomes a surfaced drive.

11. As the drive approaches a road, bear left on a path that also leads to the road. Cross the road and continue in the same direction on a path for 20 yards. Take a path on the right, which leads back to the car park where the walk started.

Walk 12
SPEARYWELL and MOTTISFONT

This short walk wends its gentle way through attractive National Trust woods and across water meadows to the village of Mottisfont, the focus of this route. The Abbey rose gardens are particularly beautiful and fragrant in June but this walk is worth doing at any time of year. While no part is strikingly dramatic or outstanding, the whole is exceptionally charming.

This teashop is very unusual in having a working post office in the corner. As well as the traditional interior, there are plenty of tables outside in the attractive garden. Clotted cream teas and a good range of delicious cakes are on offer and an unusual and tasty variant is apple scones. Light lunches of sandwiches, ploughman's or egg mayonnaise salad are served between noon and 2 pm. South African Cankwazulu and Gunpowder are among the 12 different varieties of tea that can be enjoyed here! Mottisfont Post Office Tea Rooms are open every day except Monday from Easter until the end of September between 10.30 am and 5.30 pm. They are also open on Bank Holiday Mondays. Telephone: 01794 340243.

When the teashop is closed, there is no other source of refreshment directly on the route. However, the Mill Arms in Dunbridge serves food and lies just off the route. At point 8 turn right to Dunbridge instead of crossing the road.

DISTANCE: 3¹/₂ miles.
MAP: OS Landranger 185 Winchester and Basingstoke area.
STARTING POINT: Spearywell National Trust car park (GR 316277).
HOW TO GET THERE: The car park where this walk starts is on the B3084, the Romsey to Tidworth road, about 5 miles north of Romsey at the hamlet of Spearywell.
ALTERNATIVE STARTING POINT: If you wish to visit the teashop at the beginning or end of your walk, start in Mottisfont where there are a few spots a car can be left without causing inconvenience. You will then start the walk at point 10.

THE WALK

1. Two paths leave the rear of the car park. Take the one on the left and follow the main path through woodland, ignoring paths on the left and right.

2. At a T junction with a cross path turn left.

3. At a complex junction of paths turn left then right after 10 yards on a grassy path heading gently downhill. Ignore all paths on the left and continue to a T junction with a cross path.

4. Turn left. Immediately before a wooden barrier where the path leaves the wood, turn right to stay just inside the wood. Leave the National Trust woodland at a stile and follow the path ahead. When the fence on the right ends, bear right to soon continue on a similar path. Go under the railway and carry on along the path to a bridge over a river.

5. Do not cross the bridge but go over a stile on the left into a field. The path is not very clear on the ground at the time of writing but heads half left to two wooden bridges then on in the same direction to a double stile into the next field.

6. Bear slightly right to a wire fence then walk with it on the right.

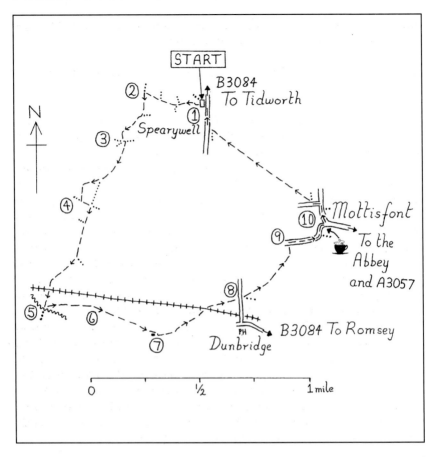

The public right of way should go round the front of an isolated thatched cottage but this route is no longer passable so continue to a gate on the right.

7. Through the gate bear left through a second gate then walk along the left-hand side of a field to a further gate. Continue along the left-hand side of the next field along an increasingly well defined track to a stile onto a level crossing. Over the crossing, follow the track to a road.

8. Cross the road, slightly left, to a stile into a field. The path, signed 'Footpath towards Mottisfont Abbey Gardens 3/4m', heads half left, gently uphill to some trees on a ridge then on in roughly the same direction to a gap in the hedge just to the left of a fine oak. Through the gap turn left on a fenced path to a lane.

9. Turn right into Mottisfont and the teashop is on the right at a junction.

In the grounds of the Abbey is a spring, which has never been known to dry up. The name Mottisfont is supposed to come from an old word for spring, 'font', and the Saxon word 'moot', meaning a meeting place - the meeting place by the spring. This is now an attractive and well-kept village, much of which is owned by the National Trust who were given the Abbey in 1957. Augustinian canons came to this gentle valley, well supplied with water and fish, at the start of the 13th century. Their foundation lasted until the Dissolution when it was given to Lord Sandys, one of Henry VIII's courtiers, in exchange for the manors of Paddington and Chelsea. Unusually, a house was constructed from the church itself rather than the domestic buildings. When the house passed to the Mills family in the 18th century it was substantially remodelled so today it is largely Georgian in appearance. It has a very interesting drawing room decorated with trompes d'oeil by Rex Whistler - the last room he painted before he was killed in the Second World War.

The rose gardens are the great glory of Mottisfont. It has an outstanding collection of old roses, moved here in 1972/3. Graham Stuart Thomas, an authority on the subject, was also the National Trust Gardens Adviser and he designed the setting - in the old kitchen garden - that makes it into a superb garden, rather than a rarefied rose museum. Many old roses have a relatively short flowering period but are heavily scented so the display is at its very best in June when the air is heady with their fragrance. To visit Mottisfont Abbey continue along the lane, past the teashop, to the entrance on the left. Telephone: 01794 41220.

10. Take the road opposite the teashop. Turn left along Bengers Lane. After 50 yards take a path on the right that heads half left across a field in the direction shown by a finger post. Continue through a narrow strip of woodland and on in the same direction to some gates and the road. Turn right, back to the start.

Walk 13
STOCKBRIDGE and the RIVER TEST

The river Test, the most beautiful of Hampshire's chalk rivers, is world famous for its trout fishing. As it wends its way towards Southampton Water, it splits into many channels that join and then divide again. This walk, the longest in this book, explores the east side of the Test valley below Stockbridge. The route is very varied, using quiet field and woodland paths, and passing through the historic village of King's Somborne. After tea in Stockbridge the first part of the return is by one branch of the river before joining the Test Way for the last couple of miles. This attractive path uses the bed of a disused railway so the walking is completely level and very easy.

Lillie Bakery and Tea Rooms on the High Street, Stockbridge is a charming traditional teashop with several tables outside overlooking a branch of the Test. The bakery on the premises produces sweet and savoury pastries as well as delicious cakes and scones. The cream teas include clotted cream. Light lunches are served between noon and 2 pm and include baguettes and croissants with a wide range of fillings. It is named after Lillie Langtry who used to visit Stockbridge in the days when nearby Danebury Racecourse still existed. It is open every day throughout the year, just closing for a couple of weeks in January. In summer the tea room is open between 9.30 am and 5.30 pm, whereas in winter it closes a little earlier at 5 pm. Telephone: 01264 810754.

DISTANCE: 8 miles.
MAP: OS Landranger 185 Winchester and Basingstoke area.
STARTING POINT: Test Valley car park, Horsebridge (GR 345304).
HOW TO GET THERE: Take a minor road signed 'Horsebridge' from the A3057 Romsey to Stockbridge road about 3 miles south of Stockbridge. The entrance to the car park is opposite the John of Gaunt.
ALTERNATIVE STARTING POINT: If you wish to visit the teashop at the beginning or end of your walk, start in Stockbridge, parking in the High Street where the teashop is to be found. You will then start the walk at point 11.

THE WALK

The very pretty hamlet of Horsebridge is at the point where the Roman road from Winchester to Old Sarum crossed the Test, though there is no sign of any Roman bridge now. The pub, the John of Gaunt, which serves excellent food, is named after the fourth son of Edward III who acquired a deer park between here and King's Somborne through his marriage to Blanche of Lancaster.

1. Return to the road and turn right then left, signed 'Kings Somborne'. After 40 yards cross a stile by a field gate on the left then walk along the right-hand side of a field to a kissing gate onto a hedged path. Follow the clearly signed path, always in the same direction, through several more gates and across fields and gardens to emerge on the A3057 through a metal kissing gate by a field gate.

2. Cross the road and take a path almost opposite, slightly left. Follow this through to a side road and turn right. When this bends right after 40 yards, turn left along a signed path. At the end of a hedge on the left, turn left then right to continue in the same direction along the edge of a playing field. At the end go through a metal kissing gate and on across a bumpy field towards a church. Take the path to the right of the churchyard to a lane.

In the days when Winchester was the capital of the realm, King's Somborne was an important place. The bumps in the field the route crosses on its way to the village are

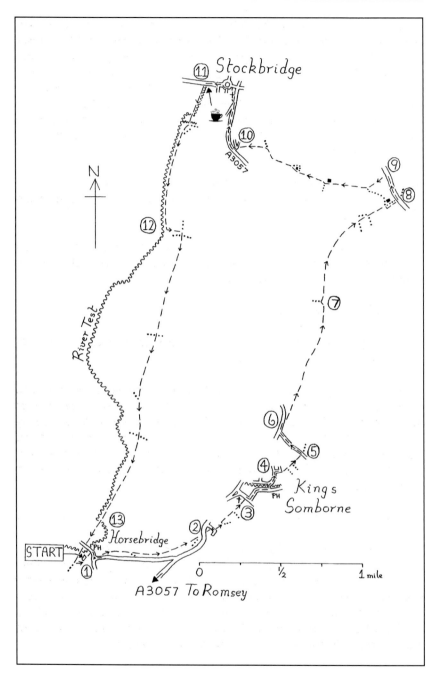

thought to be the remains of a Saxon royal palace, hence the name King's Somborne. The manor remained a royal possession before and after the Conquest and in 1190 was given to William Briwere, a faithful servant of the crown who had held many offices. Among them was Sheriff of Nottingham and he was Robin Hood's infamous adversary. One of his descendants was Blanche of Lancaster who married John of Gaunt. Their son, Henry Bolingbroke, became King Henry IV in 1399 and so the manor became a royal possession once more. The Black Death hit the village hard and with the shift of power from Winchester to London, the village sank into obscurity.

3. Turn right then take the first road on the left, signed for Little Somborne and Winchester. Just before the Andover Arms turn left along Muss Lane.

4. Take a signed footpath on the right, which soon goes to the right of a row of thatched cottages. When the houses on the right end, go ahead over a stile and across a field to a gate onto a lane.

5. Turn left to the main road.

6. Turn right for about 100 yards then take a signed path on the right along a track.

7. After about ½ mile, the main track makes a pronounced left-hand bend. At this point, fork right on a track into a wood to continue in more or less the same direction. This soon narrows to a path along the left-hand side of the wood and eventually broadens to a track again when a hedge on the left ends. Follow the track to a farm. At a cross track, just before the first barn, the path is diverted right away from the track but parallel with it to a lane.

8. Turn left for about 300 yards.

9. Turn left through a field gate along a surfaced track, signed as a footpath. At the time of writing, the stile next to the gate is extremely overgrown. Turn right at a cross track. Just past some red corrugated iron barns, bear right then continue in the same direction on a less well surfaced track towards another red barn. Take a clear path to the left of the barn to rejoin the track on the other side of the farm and continue in the same direction to the main road.

10. Turn right. On entering Stockbridge bear left to cut through the churchyard of old St Peter's then turn left into the village to the teashop on the left.

Stockbridge is an unusual village with a broad, straight main street, solidly built up on both sides with a pleasing array of buildings, mainly Tudor and Georgian, giving the impression of being the centre of a small country town. The odd thing is that there is almost nothing behind - it has been likened to a film set. The old church passed on the route is a 13th-century chancel, spared when the rest of the building was demolished in 1863.

11. Take a path immediately next to the teashop to Common Marsh, owned by the National Trust, then continue in the same direction by the river.

12. Follow the path as it bears left, away from the river to a gate. Through the gate turn right on a cross path, the Test Way. Continue on the Test Way when a track joins from the right and, at a cross track, the Clarendon Way.

The Test Way (see walk 14) and Clarendon Way are two of several long distance routes in Hampshire. From Chilbolton to Mottisfont the Test Way mainly follows the line of the old Romsey to Andover railway. Much of it was built on the bed of an old canal that linked Andover with Southampton. The waterway first came into use in 1794 but only lasted 50 years before it was superseded by the railway, which opened in 1865 and was later much used in both World Wars to move troops and supplies to Southampton Docks. The Clarendon Way is a 26 mile route linking Winchester and Salisbury.

13. Cross a bridge over the river and continue to a road. Cross the road and continue on the Test Way. Cross the river again and after a further 50 yards, turn left, back to the car park where the walk started.

The Test is famed for its trout fishing but this is not available to the general public and there are almost no footpaths along the river bank. The fishing is controlled by two exclusive and expensive clubs which were founded in the 19th century and have waiting lists for membership.

Walk 14
HAMBLEDON

Hambledon is renowned wherever cricket is played. In June 1777 the Men of Hambledon resoundingly beat the Men of All England and so ensured the village's place in history. It lies in a broad, tranquil valley explored in this attractive walk. After visiting the historic church the route heads out along the south facing slope, passing a vineyard, to the present home of the venerable cricket club. It then crosses the valley to return via the tea shop. There is some climbing, rewarded by pleasant views of rolling countryside, but the going is easy on field paths, tracks and quiet lanes. This is an ideal walk as a pipe opener in winter or for a summer's afternoon.

 The Tea Room in Lotts General Store has an attractive, cottagey décor inside a shop that sells everything from cakes through birthday cards to jam-pot covers, gardening equipment and coal. There is a display of cakes to tempt you as well as other treats on the menu such as toasted teacakes, apple pie and scones with cream. For a light lunch there is a selection of sandwiches and rolls. In summer Lotts Store has a few tables outside on a patio overlooking the road. They are open from 10 am until 4.30 pm every day (4 pm on Sunday) throughout the year. Telephone: 01705 632452.

DISTANCE: 4 miles

MAP: OS Landranger 196 Solent and the Isle of Wight and 185 Winchester and Basingstoke area.

STARTING POINT: Hambledon GR 646151.

HOW TO GET THERE: The main part of Hambledon lies just off the B2150, Droxford to Waterlooville road, and the village centre is signed from it. The village has no car park but street parking without causing inconvenience is plentiful.

ALTERNATIVE STARTING POINT: If you wish to visit the teashop at the beginning or end of your walk, start at the teashop at the southern edge of Hambledon on the B2150. There is very limited parking at the side of a small lane next to the teashop. You will then start the walk at point 8.

THE WALK

1. Make your way to the church up High Street, which is opposite a shop and not well signed. Go into the churchyard and pass to the right of the church to a lane.

Hambledon has a long history: the name is of Saxon origin and it is referred to in a charter of AD 956. The centuries are reflected in the church, which is a text book example of how an English parish church has been extended and modified from Saxon times to the present. The church expanded mainly in the 13th century when the village was granted a market. There is more information within, showing how the Saxon core can still be detected inside the present building. The extraordinary exploits of Hambledon Cricket Club in the 18th century spread the village's fame far and wide. Many of the frontages on the High Street date from this time, when a disastrous fire necessitated much rebuilding, though several of the buildings on High Street have older fragments. Tower House, on the right as you walk up High Street, was once the Red Lion and the fine metal bracket would once have held the inn sign. The smaller bracket would have held an oil street lamp.

2. Turn left then right after five yards in front of the school. At the end of the school continue ahead on a signed path between a fence and a hedge. Cross a drive and continue on a fenced path to a track.

The path leads you through Hambledon vineyard, started some 40 years ago. The grapes grown on the sunny, south-facing slopes are used to produce a fine dry white wine.

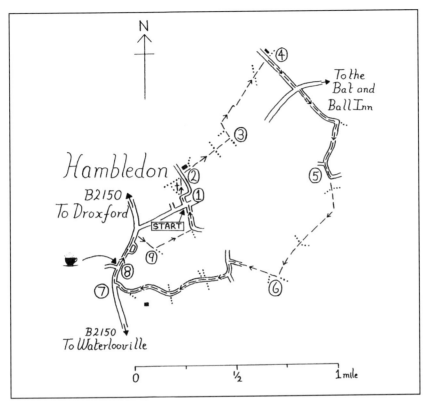

3. Turn left for 75 yards then continue uphill on a path to the left of a metal field gate to a stile into a field. Head across the field to a second stile into a copse. Follow the path on in the same direction, passing to the right of a corner fence post, to a stile onto a lane at Ridge Meadow – the present home of Hambledon Cricket Club.

The origins of cricket are lost in the mists of time but the first set of authoritative rules was drawn up in 1744 by London Cricket Club. Hambledon Cricket Club was founded in the 1750s and quickly became a force in the game. Their greatest victory came in 1777 when they beat All England at Sevenoaks by an innings and 168 runs. The match was played for 1,000 guineas in front of thousands who flocked to see sporting history being made. Memories of this famous victory are preserved in the Bat and Ball Inn, which stands opposite the ground that was then the home of the club. It lies a couple of miles to the east of the village at Broadhalfpenny Down. When the "General" of the club, Richard Nyron, moved from the Bat and Ball to the George in Hambledon, the club moved from Broadhalfpenny Down to Windmill Down, still its home. The pre-eminent position of Hambledon Cricket Club was eroded as Marylebone Cricket Club (the MCC) rose to a leading position. It is still honoured throughout the cricketing world: the President of the MCC came to open the new pavilion in 1969.

4. Turn right. Cross the main road and continue in the same direction along a lane signed 'Gliddon Farm'. Continue up through a wood, passing a lane on the right.

This is an ancient lane and the hedge on the left is a fragment of ancient woodland. Hedges are an important feature of the countryside and particularly so as refuges for wildlife. They come into existence in two ways. Some were planted – usually at the time of the Inclosure movement. Others were left as boundaries as the primeval woodland was cleared for agriculture. The one on the left of the lane was one such. It still retains the signature of its origins in the many woodland flowers such as primroses, violets and dogs mercury that bloom in spring.

5. At the top, when the lane bears left towards Gliddon Farm, continue ahead on a signed footpath along a track.

6. At a cross track turn right. The track soon becomes a lane. Turn left at a T junction and, after 80 yards, bear right at a fork.

A Roman villa once stood on the site of Bury Lodge on the left. It was uncovered when the house was rebuilt in the last century but has never been scientifically excavated.

7. Turn right along the main road to the tea shop on the left.

8. Continue along the road from the tea shop. Immediately before a terrace of painted brick and flint cottages on the right, turn right on a signed footpath. Go through a kissing gate and walk up the left-hand side of a field as far as the second gate on the left.

9. Turn left through the gate and head across two fields to a lane. Turn left back into the centre of Hambledon.

After the heyday of the village in the 18th century, agricultural depression and the Industrial Revolution reduced the population and the market ceased. William Cobbett, writing in 1826, said, "If you go through the place you can see it was a considerable town. The church tells the same story: it is now a tumbledown, rubbishy place." Fortunately, that sad comment is now also part of history and Hambledon continues into the future as a charming English village.

Walk 15
WINCHESTER

This delightful walk is of such outstanding interest - ecological, environmental, historical and literary - that it could easily take all day even though it is not particularly long or arduous. It starts with a short but stiff climb to the top of St Catherine's Hill for a wonderful view over the city with the cathedral at its heart. The route then drops down to the river Itchen and wends its way to the cathedral through lovely water meadows that inspired John Keats. Only the final couple of hundred yards are through city streets, passing in that distance the remains of a royal palace, Winchester College and Jane Austen's last home. The return leg is also by an attractive stretch of the river and is level, easy walking.

☕ Winchester Cathedral Refectory is an airy, modern building a few steps from the west door of the cathedral. It has some tables outside. The tea menu includes cream teas with clotted cream and strawberry and champagne conserve as well as a good range of tasty and delicious

69

cakes. For lunch, served from noon until 2.30 pm, a medieval custom has been given a modern twist. Food used to be served on a thick slice of bread called a trencher, which was sometimes given to the poor once the rich had eaten the topping. The idea has been brought up to date with toppings such as chargrilled courgette, tomato and mozzarella cheese. However, you are expected to eat the lot yourself! There are also sandwiches and soup and a daily selection of hot dishes. The friendly and willing service is provided by teams of volunteers from parishes within the diocese. The Refectory is open throughout the year from 9.30 am until 5 pm (4.30 pm in winter) except Christmas, New Year's Day and Good Friday. Telephone: 01962 853224.

DISTANCE: 5 miles.
MAP: OS Landranger 185 Winchester and Basingstoke area.
STARTING POINT: Garnier Road car park, Winchester (GR 484281).
HOW TO GET THERE: From the junction of the A272 and the M3 (junction 10), take the road to Winchester, the B3330. (Note: southbound you cannot leave the M3 at junction 10 so come off the motorway at junction 9 and follow the A272 to junction 10.) At the first roundabout take a road signed 'St Cross 1' for just under 1/2 mile to a car park on the left, immediately after a brick bridge.
ALTERNATIVE STARTING POINT: If you wish to visit the teashop at the beginning or end of your walk, start at Winchester Cathedral, using one of the city car parks, or the park and ride. You will then start the walk at point 11.

THE WALK
1. With your back to the entrance to the car park, take a path on the left, under a brick bridge. Bear left at a fork and follow the main path to the top of the hill.

St Catherine's Hill is a superb vantage point over the surrounding countryside. There is evidence that people lived here in the Bronze Age over 3,000 years ago but it was the Iron Age inhabitants who really left their mark. A hill fort was built in the 3rd century BC. The ramparts were far higher than those which remain today and topped with a wooden fence. A chapel dedicated to St Catherine was built on top of the hill in the 12th century and survived until the 16th century when it was knocked down following the Dissolution of the Monasteries. The rubble still forms a mound in the middle of the tree clump. The mizmaze is thought to date from the 17th century (see walk 1). St Catherine's Hill is also renowned for its flower rich turf, which supports a wide range of insect species.

2. At the top, turn right and head to the right of the mizmaze and then bear left round the hill to meet a chalky path along the ramparts

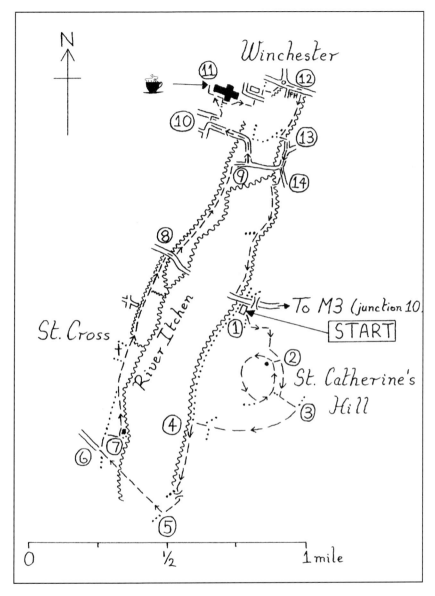

of the Iron Age fort. Turn left along it to reach the path by which you reached the top. At this point turn right along an initially overgrown path which soon becomes clear. This path is straight on if you do not go the final few feet to the top of the hill. Follow the path down into

a valley to a cross path.
(Note: at the time of writing, a direct path down into the valley from the rampart path is closed to control erosion by feet.)

3. Turn right along the bottom of the valley.

4. Go through two gates to a cross track by the Itchen Navigation and turn left. Follow the track under a bridge.

This section of the walk crosses two disused transport lines. One positive aspect of the building of the M3 is that the Winchester bypass, crossed between the two gates, has been filled in, graded and sown with suitable seeds. It is intended to nurse it back to chalk grassland. An Act of Parliament in 1665 approved the construction of the Itchen Navigation, which was completed in 1710. It ran from Winchester to Southampton and was last used as a canal in 1869.

5. As the track approaches the M3, turn right on a surfaced track to a gate. Continue along the disused road over the river Itchen and past a barrier saying 'Road Closed'.

6. Some 45 yards after the barrier, turn right on a farm drive, signed as a footpath. Follow the track round to the right.

7. Immediately before a house, turn left on a gravelled path that soon becomes a path by the river. Continue between St Cross Hospital and the river, ignoring all paths on the left. Cross a stream and continue with it on the left on a well-made path with good views across the water meadows to St Catherine's Hill.

The Hospital of St Cross was founded in 1137 by Henry of Blois, Bishop of Winchester, grandson of the Conqueror and half-brother of King Stephen, to house 13 'poor, impotent men'. After his time it declined under a succession of absentee landlords who appropriated the funds accruing from the endowments made for its support. It was rescued in the early 15th century by Cardinal Beaufort, another bishop with royal connections, being the half-brother of Henry IV, who set up his own almshouse on the same site. Elderly pensioners are still accommodated, those of the original foundation wearing black robes while those of the later establishment wear claret gowns. In Victorian times the Hospital again became notorious for administrative irregularities under an absentee master and this scandal furnished the material for Trollope's satirical novel 'The Warden'. The Wayfarer's Dole of

bread and ale has been provided to travellers for over 800 years and is still given to those who apply for it. However, do not consider this as a source of lunch as today it is just token amounts until the limited supplies run out. There are guided tours of the public rooms on weekdays.

8. At a road turn right to cross the river and then immediately left to continue in the same direction. The cathedral soon comes into view and the path passes the playing fields of Winchester College to finally emerge on a road.

John Keats visited Winchester in 1819, already sick and within 18 months of his death at the early age of 26, poor and wretchedly in love with Fanny Brawne. He walked this way to visit St Cross on a September morning and was inspired to write Ode to Autumn, 'Season of mists and mellow fruitfulness...'.

9. Turn right. At a T junction on a bend, turn left along College Walk, signed for Wolvesey Castle, the College, the Cathedral and the High Street. Pass the entrance to Wolvesey Castle (see below) then turn left along College Street.

The Black Death ravaged the ranks of the clergy as it did all sections of the population. Winchester College was founded in 1382 by the then Bishop, William of Wykeham, to provide education for 70 poor and needy scholars with the aim of providing an educated clergy. There were already schools of course, but these were always attached to a cathedral. Winchester was the first to be set up purely as an independent institution and was designed to send boys on to New College, Oxford that he had previously founded. Many of the original buildings survive.

In 1816 Jane Austen, living a few miles away at Chawton (see walk 18), fell ill with what is now thought to be Addison's disease, untreatable at the time. She came under the care of Mr Giles King Lyford of Winchester and it was decided that she should move to be near him. Accordingly, Jane made the journey with her beloved sister Cassandra in May 1817. The pair took lodgings at 8, College Street and the house is marked with a plaque. For a little while, things looked hopeful but Jane died in Cassandra's arms in the early hours of Friday 18th July and was buried in the cathedral the following week.

10. At the end of College Street turn right through some arches then right again into the cathedral precinct. Bear left, signed 'Refectory'.

The arches are one of the original gates of the city, Kingsgate, possibly of Roman origin. Above the arch is the tiny church of St Swithun, contrasting with the immensity of the cathedral close by. The cathedral houses a wealth of historic treasures too numerous to list here and a visit with a guide book is very highly recommended.

11. After tea retrace your steps to the right of the cathedral to a green on the south side. Go through an arch to the left of some columns and follow a path with first railings and then wall on the left to a gateway on the left. Go through the gate and ahead to a road opposite a car park. Turn right for 25 yards then walk up an alley on the left to the entrance to Abbey Gardens. Head for the far right-hand corner to emerge on a road by a statue of Alfred the Great. Turn right.

Winchester has an unparalleled abundance of historic buildings and is well worth taking the time to explore further. Most of the sites lie close to the centre and excellent walking tours are available from the Tourist Information Centre in the Guildhall, passed on the right (telephone: 01962 840500).

12. Immediately after the Chelsea Brewery pub turn right on a riverside path. When the path forks, bear left to cross the river in front of an imposing building that straddles the river and has a plaque which reads 'E.S. I.O.S. 1885'.

The path passes the only visible section of the Roman city walls and the remains of Wolvesey Palace can also be seen. This was built in the 12th century and was a fortified palace for the bishops of Winchester of some 40 rooms surrounding a central courtyard. It was used for several hundred years for the visits of nobility and royalty; its last great event was the wedding reception of Queen Mary and Philip II of Spain after they were married in the cathedral in 1554. Open 10 am to 6 pm daily from April until October (telephone: 01962 854766).

13. Turn right. When the road bends right, go ahead on a private road for 50 yards.

14. Take a signed path on the right which leads over the river again and along its right-hand bank to a bridge. Cross this, back to the start.

Walk 16
FREEFOLK and WHITCHURCH

Leafy lanes and quiet byways through the landscape made famous by the classic story 'Watership Down' mean this walk is a delight all year round. The route leads gently over a hill with some fine views of rolling Hampshire countryside to the ancient town of Whitchurch. On an island in the river Test is a beautifully restored and working silk mill with a teashop. Fully refreshed, your return is along the valley of Britain's purest trout stream with some more views to enjoy.

 Whitchurch Silk Mill Tearooms, Winchester Street, are on the first floor of the old building and overlook the gardens and river. The teashop is decorated with examples of how the silk from this historic mill has been used and papers are provided to read over tea. Open throughout the year every day except Monday (open on bank holidays), it serves delicious cakes and for lunch sandwiches or baguettes, filled baked potatoes and soup are offered. Please note that the enterprise is a charity and charges to look round the mill, an important part of its income. You are welcome to visit the teashop without paying the entrance charge but if you want to look round, please support their work by paying the fee. Telephone: 01256 892065.

DISTANCE: 5½ miles.

MAP: OS Landranger 185 Winchester and Basingstoke area.

STARTING POINT: St Mary the Virgin church at Freefolk. This is not the church signed from the B3400 but is immediately behind an exceptionally attractive row of thatched houses on the main road. There are several spots where a car can be left without causing inconvenience to others (GR 487488).

HOW TO GET THERE: Freefolk is on the B3400 Basingstoke to Whitchurch road. Turn down a small lane, signed as a footpath, opposite the sign to St Nicholas' church.

ALTERNATIVE STARTING POINT: If you wish to visit the teashop at the beginning or end of your walk, start in Whitchurch where there is ample parking in the car park on Winchester Street next to the mill and teashop. You will then start the walk at point 8.

THE WALK

Henri Portal was a Huguenot who fled France as a boy to escape persecution. The tradition is that he and his brother hid in an oven when the soldiers came to seize the family's chateau and they were then smuggled on board ship by servants. He established a paper mill at nearby Laverstoke, which won the contract to produce watermarked paper for the Bank of England. The hamlet of Freefolk housed the workers while the Portal family lived at Laverstoke Park, skirted by this route.

1. Continue up the lane leading to the church. In front of a house next to the church bear right up three steps and through a gate onto a surfaced path. When the surface ends, continue ahead across a field to a lane.

2. Turn right and walk along the lane, ignoring all turnings on the right. When the surface soon ends, continue ahead along the track, again ignoring all turnings on the right.

3. At a T junction with another track turn left then bear left after 10 yards. Continue on this track across a lane to a second lane.

4. Turn left, passing a lane on the left after 40 yards and continuing.

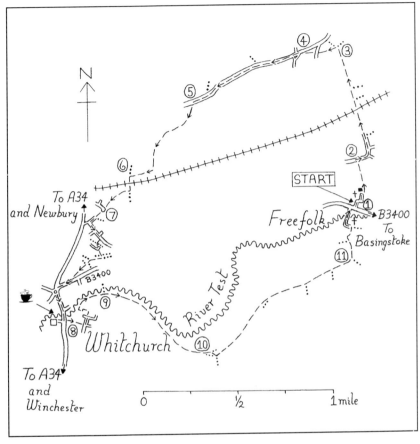

5. Some 125 yards after the drive to Wooldings Farm cross a stile on the left and walk along the left-hand side of a field. Cross a stile on the left and walk round the edge of a field, with the boundary on your left, to a farm track.

6. Turn left. Immediately after passing under the railway leave the track and cross a stile on the right. Head diagonally across a field to a stile in the far left corner to emerge at a turning circle at the end of a road.

7. Bear left along a track and continue ahead as it becomes a road. Turn left at a T junction into Lynch Hill Road. Immediately opposite number 30 take a fenced path on the right and follow this downhill into a cul-de-sac of modern houses. Bear right across the road to continue on the path downhill. At a T junction with a cross path on top of a cliff, turn right and follow the path down into Whitchurch, bearing left at a fork. Turn right along the road into the town centre. At a small roundabout turn left, following the signs to Winchester and the silk mill, on the right.

Whitchurch is an ancient town. There was a Saxon community here with a church, possibly even a minster, on the site of the present church. One of the treasures of All Hallows is the 9th-century tomb of a woman called Frithburga who was possibly a nun at Wherwell. The community grew up at an important crossing point on the river Test and in the days of horse drawn coaches bristled with inns.

At the time the Domesday Book was written, Whitchurch had four mills. One mill may have been on Frog Island where the silk mill still stands. This mill was built in 1815 as a brush factory but by the 1830s had switched to silk making which continues today. This fine industrial building has been restored by the Hampshire Buildings Preservation Trust, though the looms are now powered by electricity.

8. After visiting the mill, continue along the road and immediately after crossing the river take a walled path on the left, opposite the entrance to the car park. Follow this through to a road. Turn left. When the road bends right, continue ahead on a surfaced path that soon comes to the bank of the river Test.

9. Just before a footbridge over the river, turn right on a path along the river bank. Follow the clear path with a field on the right and then go over a stile into a small wood.

10. On emerging from the wood take a left fork to a further stile. Over this stile bear right across a field and then walk along the right-hand edge of this and the next field, climbing slightly for further wide views. St Mary the Virgin, the starting point, comes into sight.

11. At a T junction with a track turn left and walk along this, continuing when it is surfaced after passing St Nicholas' church. Cross the main road, back to the start.

Watch out for St Nicholas' church to the right of the track. Dating from the 15th century it is maintained by the Churches Conservation Trust, which cares for fine churches now surplus to requirements.

Walk 17
SHERFIELD-on-LODDON

Starting in the village of Sherfield-on-Loddon, this easy ramble explores the broad, tranquil valley of the river which gives the village its name. It is mainly on quiet field paths and almost completely level. The scenery is charming rather than dramatic with rich meadows graced by an abundance of fine trees. There are many attractive spots to linger by the river.

 The unusually named Chekato Coffee Shop at Wyevale Country Gardens occupies a light and airy corner of the garden centre with some tables outside overlooking the display gardens. There is a selection of home-made cakes to tempt you. For a light lunch there are filled baguettes or sandwiches and full meals. It is open between 9 am and 5 pm in the summer and until 4 pm in the winter. Telephone: 01256 882239.

DISTANCE: 5¹/₂ miles.

MAP: OS Landranger 186 Aldershot, Guildford and surrounding area.

STARTING POINT: The walk starts from the village car park at the junction of Reading Road and Bramley Road in Sherfield-on-Loddon (GR 679579).

HOW TO GET THERE: Sherfield-on-Loddon is signed from the A33, the Reading to Basingstoke road, about 5 miles north of Basingstoke.

ALTERNATIVE STARTING POINT: If you wish to visit the teashop at the beginning or end of your walk, there is no parking other than the garden centre car park and you should seek permission before leaving your car for a long period. The garden centre is signed from the A33. You will then start the walk at point 11.

THE WALK

1. From the junction of Reading Road and Bramley Road, walk beside the post office to a roundabout on the A33. Turn right for 50 yards then left on a signed footpath along a track.

2. A few yards after passing a house called White Gables, cross a stile over a fence on the right to continue in the same direction towards a wood. Carry on the clear path with the wood on the right then over a stream and along the left-hand side of a field to a track.

3. Turn right along the track to continue in the same direction to a farm and stay on the track, ignoring a bridleway on the right, as it bends left.

4. When the track ends at a field, head across the field then over the river Loddon and across a second field to reach a second river, the Lyde.

Geographically, this part of north Hampshire is part of the Thames Basin, being drained by rivers that flow north into the Thames. The Loddon rises about 5 miles away at Basingstoke and joins with the Lyde a couple of hundred yards north of the route. Its confluence with the Thames is near Shiplake.

5. Turn right to walk with the river Lyde on your left to a stile and bridge. Do not cross the bridge but bear right on a signed footpath to a stile and on to reach the river Loddon again. Now walk with this river on your right to a bridge.

6. Turn right over the bridge and walk along the left-hand side of a narrow field to a stile. Continue ahead for 20 yards then turn left over

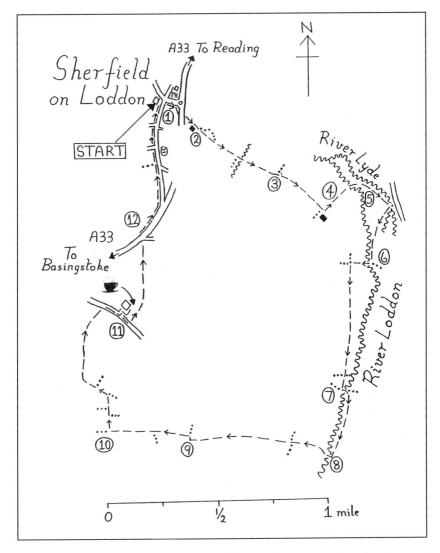

a stile. The path, which is not visible on the ground at the time of writing, goes straight ahead across two fields and over a track to reach the river bank again. Continue with the river on your left to a track which crosses the river.

7. Turn left over the bridge and then immediately right to continue along the bank with the river on your right to the next bridge.

8. Recross the river and bear half right away from the bridge to a stile beside a gate. Walk along the left-hand side of a field, cross a track and continue along the right-hand side of a large field, soon with a wood on the right. Follow the path through a narrow belt of trees and on in the same direction, shortly with a wood again on the right, and through a second belt of trees.

9. Some 25 yards after leaving the second belt of trees, cross a stile on the right into the wood. After 15 yards turn left on a clear path through the trees.

10. Immediately after a wooden squeeze stile in a fence across the path, turn right on a hedged track to join a farm track. Continue in the same direction along the farm track to reach a lane. Turn right to the garden centre and teashop.

This area is called Church End because Sherfield-on-Loddon's church lies at the junction of this lane and the A33, about a mile south of the village. One theory is that the Black Death had such a devastating effect on the population they decided to move to healthier ground. A disagreement about who could be buried in this churchyard led to a change in the law. A resident of Sherfield-on-Loddon, Baron Pigott, who was a member of the Plymouth Brethren, fell into dispute with the rector and churchwardens about whether a person who is not a member of the Church of England had the right to be buried in the parish churchyard. This led to the Burial Laws Amendment Act that states that if a person dies in a parish, even if they are just passing through, they have the right to be buried in the churchyard but only members of the established church have the right to a burial service.

11. After tea return to the lane and turn left for 150 yards. Take a signed path on the left and go straight ahead to a stile over a double fence. Over the stile, bear diagonally left across a field to a stile by a gate onto the A33.

12. Cross the road and turn right on the path by the road. After a couple of hundred yards bear left on the road into Sherfield-on-Loddon and follow it back to the start.

The move made by the village was obviously a success as this pleasant place has something of a reputation for inhabitants living to a grand old age. There is a local saying: 'You live as long as you wish in Sherfield-on-Loddon'. The village has won Hampshire's Best Kept Village competition more than once.

Walk 18
FARRINGDON and CHAWTON

In May 1811, Jane Austen wrote to her sister Cassandra, '...and the plan is that we should all walk...to drink tea at Faringdon (sic)'. This walk leads you from Farringdon to drink tea at Chawton, Jane Austen's home for the last eight years of her life. It is an easy ramble, much of it on good tracks, and the village of Farringdon is exceptionally interesting and well worth exploring. The return leg is mainly along a pleasant, level disused railway track.

Cassandra's Cup is directly opposite Jane Austen's house. It is named after Jane's sister, of course, and the sign is based on an 18th-century cup. Part of the building is modern while the rest dates back to the 18th century. Cream teas are served as well as Jane's Fancies, a tasty range of cakes and gateaux, together with other teatime goodies. Open between 10.30 am and 4.30 pm, lunch is served from noon until 2.30 pm and the daily selection of sandwiches, filled jacket potatoes, salads and hot meals is listed on a board.

It is open every day except Monday in the summer, between May and September. In the winter, it is best to phone ahead to check opening hours. Telephone: 01420 83144.

When the teashop is closed, the pub next door, the Grey Friar, serves meals.

DISTANCE: 4 miles.

MAP: OS Landranger 186 Aldershot, Guildford and surrounding area.

STARTING POINT: A parking place, marked with a blue 'P', on the A32 immediately north of Farringdon, 1¼ miles south of its junction with the A31 (GR 704354).

HOW TO GET THERE: Take the A32 Alton to Fareham road to Farringdon.

ALTERNATIVE STARTING POINT: If you wish to visit the teashop at the beginning or end of your walk, start in Chawton where there is a village car park behind the pub car park. The teashop is by the car park. You will then start the walk at point 6, taking a minor road on the left from the teashop.

THE WALK

1. Cross the A32 and take a track to Manor Farm, signed 'Right of Way', as far as a cross track.

To visit Farringdon: turn right along the cross track for 50 yards then, immediately after some wooden posts, turn left on a narrow path. At a T junction with a track, turn right. After exploring Farringdon, return to the track opposite Massey's Folly and walk along it with the church on your right. Turn left at a cross track to rejoin the route.

The most startling building in Farringdon is Massey's Folly, built in fiery red brick and terracotta. It was built by T.H. Massey who was rector from 1857 to 1919. He designed, paid for and worked on the building himself for 30 years, assisted by a bricklayer, carpenter and labourer and in the end it had 17 bedrooms. Methodism was strong in Farringdon and Massey was a dedicated opponent. He would buy up any houses with Methodist connections that came on the market and then apparently board them up. The Folly is built on the site of a house where the Methodists used to meet. No one has ever known quite why he built on such a grand and eccentric scale; local tradition has it that it was built for his mistress, said to be one Emily Parker. She was the illegitimate daughter of an Indian civil servant who lost her inheritance, came to live in Farringdon and eventually died in an institution. The building stood empty for 25 years after its completion and was then used as the village school and hall. The latter use still continues.

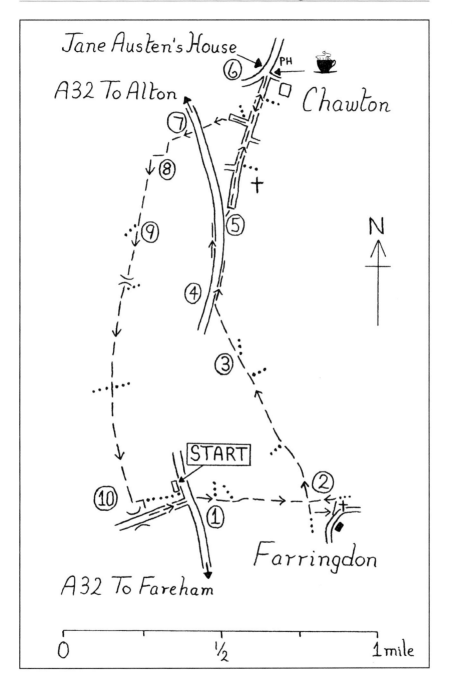

Farringdon has had a tradition of vicars serving for a long time. Gilbert White was curate here for 24 years, from 1761 to 1785, riding over from nearby Selborne (see walk 19). He was a friend of the Reverend Stephen Hales who held the living for the previous 38 years and was also of a scientific turn of mind. He was a Fellow of the Royal Society and invented a machine to ventilate the holds of ships and prisons to reduce infections. John Benn was rector from 1797 until 1857, 60 years. His eldest daughter, Harriet, was a friend of the Austens and it was the Benns with whom Jane was going to drink tea in 1811.

The 12th-century church is well worth a visit and much interesting detail is available in a guide book. It has some medieval wall paintings but unfortunately, their position is such they cannot now be seen. There are two enormous, ancient yews in the churchyard. One is reckoned to be about 3,000 years old and the other perhaps half that. Gilbert White measured the larger in 1768. When it was remeasured in 1996, it had only increased by one inch, showing how slowly yews grow. Weddings used to take place inside the larger tree.

2. Turn left, uphill. (Right if you have been to Farringdon.) Continue through a wood and on between fields and through a second small wood.

3. Immediately after leaving the second small wood, bear left to the far left-hand corner of a field to a stile onto the road.

Unfortunately, public footpaths do not always exist just where they are needed and creating new ones is a lengthy and difficult business. Ideally, the path should continue across the next field into Chawton but it does not and so we must walk round on the road.

4. Turn right. Fortunately, there is room to walk safely on the verge.

☕ **5.** Immediately after a bus stop layby on the right-hand side of the road, turn right down a surfaced path to a dead end lane. Follow the lane, passing Ferney Close on the left, into Chawton and the teashop on the right.

Jane Austen's house is opposite the teashop. Her brother Edward was adopted by wealthy and childless relatives called Knight and took their name. He inherited Chawton House, a fine Elizabethan mansion, which is now owned by an American Foundation. Jane Austen was a frequent visitor while she lived in Chawton. Nearby is St Nicholas' church. Jane's mother and much loved sister Cassandra are buried here. The church was rebuilt in 1872 after a disastrous fire. Also buried here is Sir

Edward Bradford who, according to his epitaph, was a very energetic person. He apparently served in India during and after the Mutiny, 'suppressing crime, introducing good government and popularising railways'. He also lost an arm when attacked by a tiger. Not content with his efforts in India, he became Police Commissioner in London, making the force 'a model for the world'.

Jane Austen lived in Chawton for most of the last eight years of her life. She was born and bred in Hampshire, at Steventon near Basingstoke. After living in Bath and Southampton she came to live here with her mother, Cassandra and a friend, Martha Lloyd, when her brother Edward inherited the Chawton estate and offered them all a home here. It is an unpretentious building which in those days stood at the crossroads of two main roads, the London to Winchester road and the road to Gosport. Jane did her best work here. Her only domestic responsibility was making breakfast, after that she was free to work which she did on a small table in the drawing room. This still has the legendary creaking door that warned Jane of approaching visitors. Her immediate family were well aware of what she was doing and first her father and then her brother Henry dealt with publishers for her. The house is now a museum with many interesting memorabilia of the great novelist. It is open between 11 am and 4.30 pm every day from the beginning of March to the end of December and in January and February it is open at the weekend and school half term holidays. Telephone: 01420 83262.

6. Retrace your steps to Ferney Close on the right. Walk to the end and take a path between number 1 and Ferney Bungalow then continue in the same direction along the left-hand side of a field to a stile onto the A32.

7. Cross the road and another stile and walk along the left-hand side of a field to a stile on the left into a copse.

8. At the end of the copse, turn right in the direction shown by a finger post to the end of a hedge 100 yards away. At this point turn left to the end of the field.

9. Now continue between two hedges. Go under a bridge and continue in the same direction along a track coming in from the left.

This was the Meon Valley railway line, which ran between Alton and Fareham through some lovely countryside.

10. At the next bridge take a path to the left of the bridge to a lane. Turn left, back to the start.

Walk 19
SELBORNE

*T*his outstanding walk explores the area around Selborne, which must be better described than any other parish in England. In the 18th century it was the home of the parson naturalist Gilbert White who lovingly observed and thought about the natural life he saw about him. He was in constant correspondence with others with similar interests and eventually published an edited version of his letters that has remained in print ever since. This route visits some of the places he knew through landscape which is among the finest of its sort in southern England. It starts with a steep climb up the famous zig-zag path then through beautiful beech woods before dropping down to the naturalist's home for tea. The second leg is out and back along the sides of a picturesque wooded valley, crossing the stream at the site of an Augustinian priory. Though not quite a figure of eight, it would be quite possible to do either part of the route as a shorter walk, starting or finishing along the main road through the village.

There is free admission to the Tea Parlour at Gilbert White's house, a modest charge being made for entry to the rest of this fascinating house and garden. The room used for teas is a dining room added after Gilbert White's time and it is decorated and furnished in late 18th-century style. The food is above the ordinary, being based on 18th-century recipes. The delicious cakes include lemon puffs, lemon flavoured meringues, for example. Wigs, a kind of spicy toasted teacakes, are also served. Lunch is available between noon and 2 pm and includes mushroom and chestnut pasties or egg tart. Soup and sandwiches are also served. Open 11 am until 5 pm throughout the year except Christmas week. Telephone: 01420 511275.

DISTANCE: 4 miles.

MAP: OS Landranger 186 Aldershot, Guildford and surrounding area.

STARTING POINT: Selborne village car park, behind the Selborne Arms and signed from the road (GR 742335).

HOW TO GET THERE: Selborne is on the B3006, the Alton to Liss road, and is well signed from the A3.

ALTERNATIVE STARTING POINT: There is no parking any closer to the teashop than the village car park. If you wish to visit the teashop at the beginning or end of your walk, Gilbert White's house lies to the left along the main road through the village.

THE WALK

1. Return to the entrance to the car park and take a footpath on the right, signed 'Footpath to the Zig-Zag and Hanger'. Go through a wooden kissing gate onto National Trust land and turn left, up the steps of the zig-zag path to the top. There is a seat partway up and one at the top.

This path was built by John, Gilbert White's brother. Gilbert gave help and advice and came here often.

2. Turn right on a broad path behind the seat at the top, signed 'The Common'. Ignore all side paths and continue until the wood thins on the right.

3. At a fork bear right to walk with an open area on the right, soon passing a pond on the right. At a T junction with a cross path turn left.

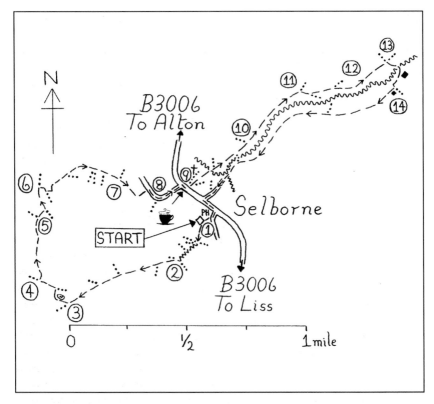

4. Turn right on a slightly downhill path by a blue topped post and follow this lovely path for about ¼ mile until a path joins on the left, again marked by a blue topped post, where there is a field on the left.

5. Continue downhill for another 50 yards. When the ground drops steeply ahead, follow the main path round to the left.

6. Just before the path climbs, turn right on a path going steeply downhill, also marked by a blue post. At the bottom turn left then shortly follow the path round to the left along the edge of the wood and ignoring turns on the right for about ¼ mile.

7. Watch for a metal gate on the right with a stile beside it. Cross the stile and walk from stile to stile along the left-hand side of several small fields to a lane.

8. Turn right to Gilbert White's house on the right at a junction.

Gilbert White was born in his grandfather's vicarage in Selborne in 1720. His family then moved away for a time before returning to live in this house, The Wakes. He was educated at Oxford, becoming a Fellow of Oriel College, and briefly held curacies elsewhere, which seems to have convinced him he preferred life in Selborne to the academic or clerical advancement he might have enjoyed. He lived the rest of his life here, serving as curate of both Selborne and Farringdon (see walk 18). His great interests were gardening and natural history, the one merging into the other. He was not particularly well off but had enough money to employ help with the labour of his gardening projects and leisure to pursue his interests.

In 1767 he was introduced to Thomas Pennant, a journalist specialising in natural history, which was very popular at the time. Pennant had a number of correspondents round the country who supplied him with news and information. Gilbert White was happy to join their number and was eventually persuaded to edit this and other correspondence for publication. However, he didn't rush to print - it took 14 years to reach the publisher and received wide acclaim. It has been in print ever since and is rightly seen as both a natural history and literary classic.

The Wakes has been extended several times since Gilbert White's day. When a public appeal failed to raise enough money to buy the house as a memorial to Gilbert White, Robert Washington Oates stepped in on condition that his family memorabilia were housed there also. Lawrence Oates was the Polar explorer who perished on Scott's expedition having uttered the immortal words, 'I am just going outside and may be some time.' Francis was his lesser known uncle who was an explorer in Africa. The Oates family had a penchant for dying on the return leg of an expedition; Francis died of a fever returning after achieving his ambition of reaching Victoria Falls.

A visit to the house and garden is strongly recommended. The garden is being restored to what it would have been in the 18th century and, thanks to White's writings, we have more information about this garden than any other at that time. The Wakes is open from mid-March until Christmas and at weekends the rest of the year. Telephone: 01420 511275.

9. Cross the open area across the road from the house. Go through the churchyard on a path signed 'Public footpath to Short and Long Lythe Hanger Way'. Leave the churchyard at a kissing gate and go ahead downhill to a footbridge then follow the path ahead along the bottom of the Short Lythe.

The green by the church is called The Plestor, which is a corruption of 'play place', and fairs and markets were held here. Gilbert White is buried under a simple headstone beside this 12th-century church, which has several interesting features including a memorial window to the great naturalist showing the 82 species of birds he mentions. Also buried in the churchyard is John Newland, known as the Trumpeter. He was leader of the local agricultural workers in 1830 and used to summon his followers with a trumpet. They attacked the workhouse, which was in Gracious Street, and so frightened the vicar that he reduced the tithes on the spot. Newland took refuge in the woods and so evaded arrest.

10. Leave the wood and follow the path into and through Long Lythe.

11. Leave the woodland through a wooden kissing gate. Bear slightly right across a meadow on a faint grassy path. After about 80 yards, before a boggy, reedy area, turn left on an even fainter path to a stile into a wood. When the path forks after 15 yards bear right.

12. Leave the wood at a further stile and continue along the left-hand side of a field to a track.

13. Turn right. Cross a bridge and continue ahead, passing a farm on the left.

The farm is on the site of a former Augustinian priory, founded in 1232 and suppressed in 1484 due to the scandalous life style of the canons. The land and property were given to Magdalen College, Oxford, which had just been founded by the then Bishop of Winchester, William Wayneflete. The buildings were used as a source of stone. The site has been excavated and some finds are on display at The Wakes.

14. Immediately before a bungalow, turn right along a track to a gate into a field. Walk along the left-hand side of two fields to a gate into a wood. Follow the track through the wood. As it leaves, it is surfaced. Continue to the road through Selborne. Turn left, back to the start.

This track, from Priory Farm to Selborne, is the old monks' way - the Via Canonorum. Gilbert White records that green hellebore is found in these woods and it is still growing here, a plant typical of beechwoods on chalk. It has small green flowers between February and April. As you approach the village, note where a cutting has exposed the underlying chalk. The tree roots can be seen penetrating into the rock, which helps break it up to form one component of the soil above.

Walk 20
QUEEN ELIZABETH COUNTRY PARK

Short and energetic, this highly recommended walk is ideal on a sunny day in spring when all around the signs of the countryside coming to life will blow away any winter cobwebs. Equally, it is outstanding in autumn when the changing vegetation makes a fiery backdrop to the landscape. Whatever the season, be sure to choose a clear day to appreciate the views, which are such an outstanding feature of this lovely route.

 The attractive modern visitor centre houses the Coach House Cafe as well as a shop and displays about the country park. The teashop has an extensive patio with picnic tables overlooking a pond. It serves a good selection of delicious cakes and biscuits and for lunch there is soup with an interesting range of sandwiches and baguettes, pasties and burgers. Open between 10 am and 5.30 pm every day from Easter to the end of October and from 10 am until dusk at weekends in the winter. Telephone: 01705 595040.

There is no alternative source of refreshment on this walk.

DISTANCE: 4½ miles.
MAP: OS Landranger 197 Chichester and The Downs.
STARTING POINT: Halls Hill car park (GR 733198).
HOW TO GET THERE: From the A3 south of Petersfield take a minor road, signed 'Buriton' coming from the north and 'Petersfield' from the south. Follow this to Buriton then take a lane on the right, signed 'Chalton 4 Finchdean 6', to Halls Hill car park on the right.
ALTERNATIVE STARTING POINT: If you wish to visit the teashop at the beginning or end of your walk, start at the visitor centre (signed from the A3) where there is ample parking. The teashop is in the visitor centre. You will then start the walk at point 4.

THE WALK

1. Leave the car park by the broad track at the far end and follow it uphill. As you climb, extensive views to the north-east open up behind you - well worth pausing to enjoy!

Queen Elizabeth Country Park covers 1,400 acres of the western end of the South Downs. It is part of the East Hampshire Area of Outstanding Natural Beauty and after this walk I am sure you will agree with that designation! It covers three hills: War Down and Holt Down are wooded and visited on this route. Butser Hill is covered with chalk grassland and there are magnificent views across to it shortly. The park is managed jointly by Hampshire County Council and Forest Enterprise.

2. Soon after the track levels out, turn sharp right, almost back on yourself, on another wide track. When this track forks after 180 yards, bear left, continuing uphill. After a pronounced left-hand bend, continue ahead, passing a wide path on the left, and ignore all paths and tracks to both left and right until you approach a parking area.

Left alone, without any human interference, these hills would be covered by forest with many yews. This environment is so suitable for yews that they are sometimes called the Hampshire weed. Yew is a long lived conifer that can survive for hundreds and even thousands of years and grow to immense size. The tree has never been popular with farmers because all parts of the plant are poisonous. On the other hand, the wood is very strong and was used for making the famous long bows of England. Due to these conflicting demands, yews are mainly found in churchyards. The woodland on this walk is quite modern. The beech and conifer

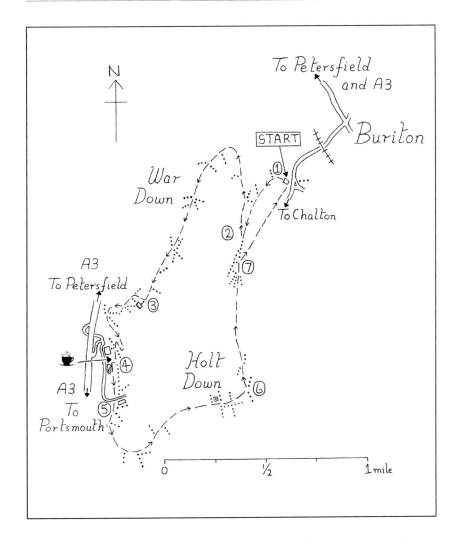

woodlands on *War Down* and *Holt Down* were planted in the 1930s to help meet the country's timber needs. They are still managed commercially so this is a working landscape as well as being very beautiful. However, yews, juniper (easily recognised by its distinctive gin smell) and other species can be found among the beech and remnants of dark green yew woodland can be seen on Butser Hill across the valley.

Butser Hill is the highest point of the South Downs and well worth visiting for its outstanding views. It is less wooded and the open chalk downland, with its wealth of wild flowers, is maintained by a flock of sheep. Without their grazing, nipping off *the growing point of all tree seeds that germinate, the hill would soon be invaded by scrub and would eventually become covered with forest again. There are signs of ancient human activity on Butser Hill - Iron Age field boundaries on the lower slopes and defensive works on the summit.*

3. Immediately before the parking area, opposite a display area with boards explaining the management of the forest, turn right across an open area with children's play equipment to meet a cross path at the far side. Turn left. At a cross path turn right downhill and follow this path across a track and on down to the visitor centre.

As you descend, the sylvan tranquillity is increasingly disturbed by the noise of the traffic on the A3 below. The A3 is in a deep cutting here which at least allows a glimpse of the underlying chalk. It is this geology that is the fundamental cause of this outstanding landscape. The chalk was laid down at the bottom of the sea millions of years ago and later pushed up into folds by the same earth movements that built the Alps.

4. Leave the teashop along a path signed 'Hangers Way' and 'Staunton Way' with the pond on your right.

These two long distance paths both start at Queen Elizabeth Country Park. Staunton Way runs 12 miles south to Langstone Harbour while Hangers Way goes north for 21 miles to Alton.

5. Cross a surfaced drive to a track signed 'Staunton Way'. Follow this uphill, bearing left at a fork. Bear left again at the top of the hill. Continue on the main track, passing a fenced pond on the left. Soon after this the track starts to descend.

6. At an obvious cross track turn left, uphill again, soon passing a Hangers Way sign on the left.

7. After about ½ mile, turn right on a clear path, signed 'Hangers Way', and follow this out of the woods and across fields, back to the start.
(Note: if using the alternative start continue ahead for about 200 yards instead of turning right at point 7, to pick up the route at point 2, forking left.)